$4.00

Vogt Memorial

1962-1963

The life of Lewis Henry Morgan,
who founded the science of anthropology, has been described as one of the
strangest in American intellectual history. Lawyer d politician, entr
neur in d mi
and c
Pr
m

inv

t

LEWIS HENRY MORGAN
AMERICAN SCHOLAR

LEWIS HENRY MORGAN
AMERICAN SCHOLAR

By Carl Resek

THE UNIVERSITY OF CHICAGO PRESS

Library of Congress Catalog Number: 60-5468

THE UNIVERSITY OF CHICAGO PRESS, CHICAGO 37
Cambridge University Press, London, N.W. 1, England
The University of Toronto Press, Toronto 5, Canada

© *1960 by The University of Chicago. Published 1960*

For KATE

PREFACE

Lewis Morgan's story, Professor Ralph Gabriel has suggested, is one of the strangest in American intellectual history. It is that. No other American in his own time or since has looked on human society in quite the manner that Morgan did, and few have wandered down the paths of scholarship that he charted. He fits no customary interpretation of the nineteenth-century mind and will not allow any tidy explanation of his views or motives. Some writers have called him a conservative Social Darwinist, though he deeply suspected that body of doctrine and only partially understood it. Passing over his fervent career as a Whig and Republican politician, other scholars have thought him a spokesman of socialism. Some cite his *magnum opus* as a defense of American capitalism, although it contains the severest censures of the profit motive. A few view Morgan as an apologist for imperialism. But he supplied the strongest single argument against the white man's burden philosophy. His mind, in short, cannot be pinned down nicely without being divested of its rich and many-sided character.

Morgan created the science of anthropology. Because he paid little heed to established methods of inquiry and became a thoroughly unorthodox thinker, he has remained a controversial one. What follows is not an attempt to rehabilitate his theories, which have suffered badly in the light of twentieth-century anthropology. His work must be evaluated by those trained in the field. But the historian needs to account for the origins of Morgan's ideas and for the decline of their influence. Charles Darwin, after all, thought him the New World's first social scientist. Francis Parkman called Morgan his mentor, and Henry Schoolcraft declared him the greatest Indian authority in the land. Henry Adams viewed his work as the "foundation of all future American historical scholarship." To Friedrich Engels he was worth a full volume. Andrew D. White invited him to teach at Cornell, and Harvard's Charles Eliot Norton asked him to direct archeological research in the American southwest. Who, then, was Lewis Morgan?

The answer can only be partial. A large portion of Morgan's papers were destroyed, either by himself or, shortly after his death, by Mrs. Morgan. Most of his personal history is shrouded in darkness and only a part of his legal, business, and political career has come to light. But, fortunately, he left his manuscripts and less personal letters to the University of Rochester, and from these, together with materials in other archives, the main narrative of his life can be reconstructed. Primarily they yield insight into the body of principles that guided his mind through the variety of its adventures. To uncover the assumptions that men live by in another time or place and that they modify or exchange for others as experience demands seems the initial task of intellectual history. Morgan, whose doctrines were hailed by Americans in one century and discarded by them in the next, may be a measure of the changes in American life and thought during these years.

I am indebted to Richard C. Wade and Glyndon G. Van Deusen of the University of Rochester for guiding me through the first phase of this study and to Charles Vevier for aiding its publication. David Donald, Bert J. Loewenberg, Leslie A. White, and Robert Wiebe read the manuscript and suggested numerous improvements. Margaret Butterfield, Saul Benison, Temple Hollcroft, and the late

Bernhard J. Stern helped me through several intricacies in Morgan's history. The Columbia University Council for Research in the Social Sciences aided me financially in the completion of the book. Thanks, most of all, to my wife, Kate Frances Resek.

CONTENTS

CHAPTER I

SEEDS OF DOCTRINE

Lewis Morgan was twenty years old when he added Henry to his name and rode out of his native village of Aurora to attend Union College in Schenectady. The year was 1838 and the Finger Lakes country was in its autumn glory. Among the neighboring Iroquois it was said that the Great Spirit pressed his hand into the earth here and caused rain-waters to fill the valleys he had made. An engaging picture, it seemed no more difficult to believe than that half a million years ago a vast ice sheet, pressing down from the north, gouged out five channels and, melting, turned them into lakes.

For a century and a half after their arrival in the New World, Lewis' New England ancestors heard reports of this lake country and its hardwood forests thick with elk, deer, and beaver, of its boundless rolling meadows with the heaviest vines and bluest skies yet seen. But when their own land grew scarce and younger sons pushed west, they passed by the lakes and settled inland. To the south, Scotch-Irish farmers looked enviously across the Susquehanna Valley to the fertile northern country, but they also declined to settle it, and turned to Virginia instead. Americans fought at Bunker Hill before the first ax echoed across the Finger Lakes.

The five tribes of the Iroquois were an impenetrable barrier. About twelve thousand strong and living in dozens of villages west of the Hudson, they were a sedentary people who knew farming, as well as hunting and grazing. They carried on commerce with white men, trading furs for arms and implements, but turned into fierce warriors when settlers threatened their domains. Pioneer villages in the Mohawk Valley were wiped out repeatedly until the reports of slaughter and destruction stayed all advance into western New York. During the Revolution the Iroquois joined the British to fight land-hungry Americans, adding to the fury of Yankee and Scotch-Irish farmers. Five thousand of these descended on the Iroquois in the summer of 1779 and, in a swift campaign under Generals Clinton and Sullivan, broke their power. Within ten years the Indians surrendered their lands in return for small payments and reservations and began their career as subjects of ethnological inquiry.[1]

Through the opened floodgates came a torrent of settlers from the east and south. Five hundred sleds passed through Albany in a day headed for western New York, and in spring and summer even heavier traffic swelled the Mohawk. At the request of Congress the state set aside most of the Finger Lakes country as a military tract reserved for land payments to veterans of the Revolution in lieu of cash. Though many soldiers promptly sold their deeds, the tract was well settled by the turn of the century. Among those who took possession of their claims was Lewis' grandfather, Sergeant Thomas Morgan of New London, Connecticut, whose five years of service in the Continental Army, including several weeks west of the Hudson under General George Clinton, entitled him to a six-hundred-acre lot.[2]

---

[1] Frederick W. Hodge (ed.), *Handbook of American Indians North of Mexico* (Washington: Government Printing Office, 1907), I, 618–19; Alexander C. Flick, "The Sullivan-Clinton Campaign of 1779," *History of the State of New York*, ed. A. C. Flick (New York: New York State Historical Association, 1933), IV, 185–216; Lewis H. Morgan, *League of the Ho-de-no-sau-nee or Iroquois* (Rochester: Sage & Bros., 1851), pp. 3–35.

[2] Jeannette B. Sherwood, "The Military Tract," *Quarterly Journal of*

Thomas and his family set out for New York in the spring of 1792. In an ox-drawn wagon they made their way to Utica by turnpike and from there, alternately on barges and by Indian trails, up the Mohawk Valley through Oneida Lake to Lake Cayuga, settling at Scipio, near its eastern bank. Thomas was fifty years old then but worked his new farm for another twenty-three. A tough, pious Presbyterian, he gave his offspring such names as Prudence, Temperance, Ephraim, and Jedediah. A family legend had it that he moved west to keep his sons off the sea and on the farm. If so, he failed. His eldest stayed behind to become a ship's captain, and another soon returned to New London to sail for the Indies.[3]

The third son, Jedediah, Lewis' father, was eighteen when the family arrived at Scipio. He helped Thomas clear timber and build a homestead, then tended a growing flock of sheep whose wool brought a dollar a pound at neighboring markets. But he too preferred the water and moved a few miles west to Aurora, a thriving lake port to which Cayuga farmers shipped their produce on its way east. He engaged in "mercantile pursuits," tinkered with a few improvements on the plow, a national pastime in those days, and built a trim home overlooking the lake. Married at twenty-four, he was a widower at thirty-one and the fa-

the *New York State Historical Association*, VII (1926), 169–79; Henry M. Allen, "A Story of Cayuga County," *Archaeological Society of Central New York Bulletin*, IX (April, 1954), 47–51; Lois K. Mathews, *The Expansion of New England* (Boston: Houghton Mifflin & Co., 1909), pp. 153 ff.

[3] For a history of the Morgans see Nathaniel H. Morgan, *A History of James Morgan of New London, Connecticut, and His Descendants* (Hartford: Lockwood & Brainard, 1869), and J. Appleton Morgan, *A History of the Family of Morgan from the Year 1089 to the Present* (New York: Privately printed, 1897); also Connecticut Historical Society, *Collections*, VIII (1901), 216; Henry P. Johnston (ed.), *The Record of Connecticut Men in the Military and Naval Service during the War of the Revolution, 1775–1783* (Hartford: Case, Lockwood & Brainard Co., 1889), pp. 250, 451, 587.

ther of five. His second wife, Harriet Steele of Hartford, Lewis' mother, bore him eight children more.[4]

Jedediah grew wealthy in other ways. By 1820 the family farm consisted of seven hundred acres worked by tenants or sold at twenty-five dollars an acre. A substantial herd of cattle and several thousand sheep grazed on it. Friends thought Jedediah a respectable farmer, while some called him a village aristocrat. His name grew familiar in the lake country, and in 1823 he was elected state senator and told to push the construction of internal improvements, especially the Erie Canal. As a member of the Senate's Committee on Agriculture he made no mark, but he gained fame in Albany as one of three senators to vote against DeWitt Clinton's removal from the Canal Commission. Cayuga farmers revered Clinton for his championship of the canal, and to disgrace him at the bidding of eastern politicians was unthinkable. Besides, Clinton, the foremost Freemason in the state, had laid the cornerstone of Jedediah's lodge. Albany gossips whispered about Senator Morgan's secret oaths to his leader. But in the presidential election of 1824, to their surprise, Morgan supported John Quincy Adams, no friend of Clinton, or of the Masons. The Senator, his colleagues concluded, was a true and "warm Federal." [5]

When he died, in December, 1826, after a lingering illness, his son Lewis was eight. The three oldest boys, Jed,

<hr/>

[4] S. R. Harlow and S. C. Hutchins, *Life Sketches of State Officers, Senators and Members of the Assembly of the State of New York in 1868* (Albany: Weed, Parsons & Co., 1868), pp. 103–4; Cyrenus Wheeler, "The Inventors and Inventions of Cayuga County," Cayuga County Historical Society *Collections*, II (Auburn: Knapp & Peck, Printers, 1882), 115.

[5] Jedediah Morgan, "Last Will and Testament," July, 1820, probated April 28, 1827, in Surrogate's Court of Cayuga County, Auburn, New York; *Auburn Free Press*, October 20, November 17, 1824, December 27, 1826; *Albany Argus and City Gazette*, April 25, 1824, November 12, 1824, November 25, 1826; *Journal of the Senate of the State of New York*, 48 Sess., 1825, *passim*.

William, and Amos, assumed management of the farms, while Harriet took charge of the household in Aurora and raised the younger children, including twin daughters just ten months old. Jedediah had left them all well provided. But Lewis had not been ready for the parting.[6] He grew up in a restless frontier town, and, learning its rules alone, he sometimes made a lifeline of them. The new canal left nothing the same. Daily, neighbors moved to one of the new towns in the north, Syracuse, Rochester, Batavia, and Buffalo. On the post road that passed before his house pioneers headed west, and one day Amos announced he was starting for Illinois. Soon after, William left for Kentucky. Even in the meetinghouse where his father had purchased a pew and slip no one stayed put. Visiting ministers shouted a great deal as people fell on their knees, sobbing. No minister ever persuaded Lewis to do the same.[7]

But there were sights that had made a boy marvel. From his window, boats laden with sacks of grain, wool, and lumber could be seen coming into port or passing by on their way to New York, their goods destined for some distant city by the sea. On the other side of the village the forest held an abundance of treasures. The gnawed branches of a raspberry bush and stumps of maple marked the presence of beaver; if one learned to walk softly upstream, they might be caught at work. There were rabbits and snakes, minerals and fossils in the ravines, and arrowheads

[6] "But a child is never ready to part with a parent. You were fortunate to have a father through so long a period of your life." Morgan to Eben Horsford, February 16, 1875, Morgan MSS, Rush Rhees Library, Rochester. This collection, which supplied the major portion of source material for this biography, is hereafter cited as "Morgan MSS."

[7] For the religious enthusiasms in western New York see Whitney R. Cross, *The Burned-over District* (Ithaca: Cornell University Press, 1950); also James H. Hotchkin, *A History of the Purchase and Settlement of Western New York and of the Rise, Progress, and Present State of the Presbyterian Church in That Section* (New York: M. W. Dodd, 1848). For Morgan's reaction, see below, chap. iii.

that made threadbare tales of Red Jacket and Chief Joseph Brant come alive. Lewis Morgan was a grown man before he stopped imagining "the day when the forest cast its shadow over the lake and the Indian with his bow and arrow pursued his game to the water's edge and along its winding banks; when that stillness of the wood unknown to us was unbroken even by the Indian hunter, save now and then by the twang of the bow string, the whizzing of an arrow, or the whoop indicating victory in the chase." [8]

Jedediah had set aside a fund for his education. In the Aurora schoolhouse Lewis learned to read and write, and when he was sixteen, he enrolled in the Aurora Academy. Not ten years after they settled in Aurora, Yankees built the academy to insure the education of their sons. In the stately brick building overlooking the bay, Lewis studied Latin and Greek, read Cicero and Herodotus, and learned principles of rhetoric and mathematics. He grew fond of his studies and of his fellow students. A common interest, he learned, was the beginning of companionship, and he organized a club "for the purpose of mutual improvement in useful knowledge." Every Friday evening his Erodephecin Society, some fifteen members in all, met to debate weighty matters and applied the rules of rhetoric indispensable to future servants of the Republic. Lewis loved the ring of a proud phrase rolling across the lectern to the audience and drew satisfaction from a well constructed argument. He decided to study law and, upon taking an examination, was admitted to the junior year at Union. [9]

Established in 1795 as the first non-sectarian college in the

[8] Morgan to G. S. Riley, December 12, 1845, Morgan MSS.

[9] *Celebration at Cayuga Lake Academy, July 22, 1857* (New York: F. Hart, Printer, 1857); George F. Miller, *The Academy System of the State of New York* (Albany: J. B. Lyon & Co., 1922); Morgan, "Erodephecin Society, Constitution and By-Laws and a List of Members," n.d., Morgan MSS.

country, the school derived its name from the union of all faiths on its board of trustees, the majority of whom could not at any one time be composed of the same sect. In 1804, Reverend Eliphalet Nott, pastor of the First Presbyterian Church of Albany, having just delivered his most famous sermon, "Occasioned by the Ever to be Lamented Death of General Alexander Hamilton," left his pulpit to become Union's president. Since then he had transformed the small and debt-ridden college into one of the nation's leading centers of higher learning.

Lewis Morgan enjoyed himself at Union. From the first, he was a serious student, worked assiduously, and was rewarded with high marks. He attended lectures in mechanical science and mathematics and was tutored in Greek, Latin, Italian, and political economy. He took part in school debates and won distinction for his oratorical talents. The idea of organized brotherhoods, then very popular at Union, made a lasting impression on him when he was elected to a Greek-letter fraternity. But the most permanent influence on him was that of Dr. Nott, whose lectures he attended in the first semester of the senior year and with whom he got along extremely well.

Nott was the Yankee personified, whose talent for practical matters seemed boundless. The Nott stove was the most successful of his many inventions, and Nott and Company were the leading stove manufacturers of the day. He made investments in iron and copper mines and managed a lottery to raise funds for his college. He gained respect and influence among Albany's hardy politicians, who frequently came to his aid. This worldly bent—William Henry Seward, one of Union's most eminent graduates, called it "manly"—pervaded the entire school. "I think I know of no institution where a manlier spirit prevailed among the undergraduates than that which distinguishes the pupils of

Dr. Nott," Seward recalled. None of this was at the expense of the faith. The president insisted that every student have a thorough grounding in the Old and New Testaments. But he also believed that a knowledge of God was best acquired from the study of His material creations. To know the laws of nature, he told his pupils, is to know God's rules which illuminate the mind and cleanse the spirit. Like Jonathan Edwards, he thought revealed and natural religion identical and strengthened alike in church and school. Thus, he preached to some of the largest revival meetings in western New York while he laid plans for the founding of Rensselaer Polytechnic Institute. More room was given to instruction in the sciences at Union, and a strictly classical curriculum gave way to a modified elective system. "I care less for Greek than you do," he told the popular classics instructor, Taylor Lewis, "and less for books generally, as a means of educational discipline." [10]

As in most American colleges of the day, the president's lectures were the crowning part of an education at Union. And, as elsewhere, they were designed to indoctrinate the graduating class with a sound public philosophy whose prime ingredient was moral science. The Newton of moral science was Lord Kames, the Scottish jurist and friend of Benjamin Franklin, whose *Elements of Criticism* was the text for Nott's course. Kames emphasized empirical learn-

---

[10] W. H. Seward, *An Autobiography*, ed. Frederick W. Seward (New York: Derby & Miller, 1891), p. 29; Seward and Morgan knew each other in their youth according to Morgan to Henry R. Schoolcraft, April 29, 1849, Morgan MSS. On Nott see Codman Hislop, "A Loud and Awful Warning," *New York Historical Society Quarterly*, XL (1956), 5–19; Joseph Rotundo, "Eliphalet Nott," *New York History*, XIII (1932), 166–73; Dixon R. Fox, "Dr. Eliphalet Nott and the American Spirit," *Newcomen Address, 1944* (Princeton: Princeton University Press, 1944); C. Van Santvoord, *Memoirs of Dr. Nott* (New York: Privately printed, 1875); Nott to Morgan, November 8, 1841, Morgan MSS; Bernhard J. Stern, *Lewis Henry Morgan, Social Evolutionist* (Chicago: University of Chicago Press, 1931), p. 5.

ing and the importance of observation and experience as the fountains of human values. Absolutes were the results, not the beginning, of scholarly investigations; knowledge a product of the senses as well as of reflection. This Lockian discipline banished from Union College all forms of doubt about the reality of subjective perceptions and all ideals not grounded in the laws of nature. Common sense was the queen of Nott's philosophy, and her outcasts included James I, Bishop Berkeley, Charles Fourier, William Lloyd Garrison, and Andrew Jackson. The former pastor exhorted his seniors to go out into the world with open eyes, see how it functioned, and accept its iron laws.[11]

And so they did. Alonzo Potter, one of his best pupils and his successor as president of Union, declared in 1840 that trade unions were harmful because they were contrary to the laws of God and nature. Private property, wrote the equally renowned graduate of the college and later president of Brown University, Francis Wayland, was founded in "the will of God as made known to us by natural conscience, by general consequence and by revelation." To the future lawyers in Nott's classroom, Chancellor Kent's dictum that "the law as a science is only a collection of general principles founded on the moral law and in the common sense of mankind," was common sense itself.[12] When they went into politics, as many of them did, Union graduates were usually Whigs guarding the Republic against Locofoco disorder.

[11] Helen W. Randall, "The Critical Theory of Lord Kames," *Smith College Studies in Modern Languages*, XXII, Nos. 1-4 (October, 1940, to July, 1941); Woodbridge Riley, *American Thought from Puritanism to Pragmatism* (New York: Henry Holt, 1923), pp. 118-22.

[12] Henry F. May, *Protestant Churches and Industrial America* (New York: Harper & Bros., 1949), p. 15; Francis Wayland, *The Elements of Moral Science* (Boston: Gould, Kendall & Lincoln, 1850), p. 229; James Kent, *An Address Delivered before the Law Association of the City of New York, October 21, 1836* (New York: G. & C. Carvill, 1836), p. 8.

But a Hamiltonian sense of progress graced such Whiggery. Nott nurtured it with François Guizot's *History of Civilization in Europe*. When Morgan arrived at Union, the French historian and constitutional monarchist was just beginning his eight fateful years as chief minister to Louis Philippe, drawing still more attention to a book already popular in American colleges. Guizot washed the taint of the French Revolution off the idea of progress together with the marks of such rationalists as Turgot and Condorcet. Progress to him was implied in the word civilization, and its chief agency was a stable middle class that meliorated the social system by the expansion of trade, industry, and education. The commercial revolution brought improvements that the social never fathomed. The good burgher in Paris as in Schenectady was duty bound to serve mankind by serving himself. All this made eminent sense at Union. For the commercial boom that transformed western New York in the years after the completion of the Erie, the college supplied lawyers, commissioners, engineers, experts in metallurgy, trigonometry, banking, hydrostatics, and international trade. When the boom was over, many of its graduates moved west and took part in the process of building up new regions.

That was what Lewis Morgan hoped to do. Once admitted to the bar, he would leave the provinces and share in the great tide of progress that had passed Aurora by, just fifty miles to the north. He would find his station somewhere along the "Great Ditch" between Albany and Buffalo or move to some thriving inland city. Nott inspired him no more than Schenectady's sawmills, tanneries, grist mills, and forges or the million barrels of wheat that floated through the city each year. Morgan was confident he would make his mark. "We all know the vast superiority that an educated has over an uneducated mind," he told students at

Aurora Academy on his return. The intellect was a tool, indeed it was wealth, in a country so full of opportunity.[13] His mind's capital made him conservative and, Aurora's schoolboys must have thought, somewhat haughty. In April, 1840, he took leave of Union for the spring semester and returned to Aurora, where he arrived just in time to hear Henry C. Wright of the Boston Non-Resistance Society, deliver a lecture. Wright's group, dedicated to ending war by passive resistance, also advocated the abolition of slavery. Morgan listened patiently to the speaker, then hurried home and penned a reply that he delivered at the academy three days later.[14]

"This is emphatically an age of humbuggery, of fanaticism and of nonsensical schemes, an age of violent denunciation from the self-righteous," he declared. Scarcely a day passed but that reason and judgment were assailed by reformers expounding human perfectability, the idleness of laws, and the iniquity of government. He had no patience with such views. Non-resistance was plain sedition because a nation that could not depend upon the allegiance of its citizens must surely fall into the depth of barbarism. Was the United States to be destroyed by English arms or go down in the "horror of noctural massacres at the hands of savages" for the sake of such doctrines? As for the aboli-

[13] Morgan, "Essay on Geology, June 7, 1841, delivered at the Aurora Academy," Morgan MSS; on Guizot see J. B. Bury, *The Idea of Progress* (New York: Dover Publications, Inc., 1955), pp. 260–77; A. A. Ekirch, *The Idea of Progress in America, 1815–1860* (New York: Columbia University Press, 1944), pp. 1–105. Frederick L. Bronner, "Union College and the West," *New York History*, XXX (1932), 173–79. Paul Kosok (ed.), "Lewis Henry Morgan on the Flour Mills and Water Power of Rochester," *Rochester Historical Society Publications* (hereafter cited as "*RHSP*"), XXIII (1946), 109–27, illustrates how Morgan related the idea of progress to the Erie's commerce.

[14] "An Address on Non-Resistance Delivered before the Members of the Aurora Lyceum," April 7, 1840, Morgan MSS. On Wright see Merle Curti, *The American Peace Crusade, 1815–1860* (Durham, N.C.: Duke University Press, 1929), pp. 74–85.

tionists, though slavery was a disgrace, so were "prayers for Christian Charity and Toleration by the same men who declare their southern fellow-citizens to be thieves and robbers, yes unblushingly call them miscreants and vagabonds and every vile epithet that malignant animosity can suggest . . . because they hold slaves which their laws sanction and permit."

Passions subsiding, he drove more tempered shafts. He described government as a necessary safeguard to public order and private property, and as an instrument of commercial expansion. In truth, it behooved the United States to build a strong navy for the protection of overseas trade and to use its armies in the acquisition of western lands. The state rested on the power to enforce its will, and to repudiate it for the sake of higher precepts was unthinkable. Indeed, where find these alternate and higher laws? "Take our abolitionists. They profess to follow the precepts of the Bible as strictly and as purely as the Non-Resister does; but here we see that the same Bible sets two societies at war; it tells one not to meddle in politics and the other that it is his imperative duty to do so."

Years later, when he reread this speech, Morgan marked it as a product of youthful exuberance. Still, it contained doctrines that he adhered to through much of his life, and the urgency with which he later questioned them gave evidence to their tenacity. But even now a careful observer might have noted that the young scholar protested too much and suspected that such copious realism subdued a full-blown romantic.

After finishing the third semester of his senior year, Morgan delivered the class valedictory, a discourse on the common law.[15] He considered taking a grand tour of Europe

[15] No copy of it is extant. Dixon R. Fox to Bernhard J. Stern, April 15, 1936, Stern Papers in the possession of Mrs. Bernhard Stern, New York City.

but gave it up for lack of funds and decided instead to finish reading law. Between long hours over Blackstone, Coke, Story, and Kent, he studied Hebrew at the academy, taught Latin, and every so often delivered a lecture at the village lyceum.

Within a few months he was admitted to the bar, but it was three years before he found employment. The Panic of '37, though not as severe in western New York as elsewhere, produced a surplus of young lawyers. Morgan made occasional trips across the state in search of a position, but with no success. In Rochester, he was told, there was less business waiting for lawyers than lawyers for business, and replies from other towns were equally discouraging. Not to be able to employ one's talents was exasperating. The human intellect, he decided, contains an impulse to action, a desire for employment: "we live as well to act as to think." [16]

He helped manage the family farms and read what books were available in Aurora. It was a meager diet, and years later he made up for it by building one of the largest private libraries west of the Hudson. Now he translated Horace, studied state and federal reports, read Shakespeare, Irving, Cooper, and worn copies of the *Knickerbocker*. At the lyceum he heard a variety of lecturers, advocates and prophets for most of whom he had no use. But he was impressed by the temperance crusaders, whose sermons he had listened to and read in the *Auburn Free Press* since child-

[16] "The year 1842 found me in Aurora admitted as an attorney but not yet ready from the depression of all business to commence practice." "Record of Indian Letters . . . 1859," I, Morgan MSS; Timothy Childs to Morgan, February 6, 1843; Erastus Corning to Morgan, February 16, 1844, Morgan MSS; Samuel Rezneck, "The Social History of an American Depression," *American Historical Review*, XL (1935), 662-87; Walter B. Smith and Arthur H. Cole, *Fluctuations in Business, 1790-1860* (Cambridge, Mass.: Harvard University Press, 1935), pp. 64-79; Blake McKelvey, *Rochester the Water-Power City 1812-1854* (Cambridge, Mass.: Harvard University Press, 1945), pp. 213-21.

hood. Temperance contained a whole philosophy, as Dr. Nott had shown at Union. It had economic and patriotic implications and explained in part why the beneficent laws of nature were not functioning in the present crisis. He wrote three lectures on the subject and sought invitations from lyceums in neighboring villages.

During the summer of 1842 and in the following year, Morgan campaigned, among other places, in Aurora, Geneva, Springport, Scipio, and Auburn. Gravely he demonstrated that liquor injures the body, the soul, and especially the moral sense. "Misery and wretchedness, and the folly and crimes in society are, in the great proportion of cases, either directly or indirectly the consequence of intemperance." The business depression itself was related to it. Alcohol caused neglect, supplied no economic want; it didn't clothe the needy or feed the hungry. "Export this trash for sale in foreign markets. It would pay our debts abroad and returning prosperity would again bless this fair Republic." In the meantime sober and industrious farmers should not be taxed to support city paupers and criminal courts. Temperance would do away with both.

In all probability intemperance caused the ruin of empires. The most sublime discovery of the ancients, Morgan explained, was that the laws of nature were perfect and unchangeable and man's only guide through life. Adherence to them was his guaranty of safety; departure invited injury. They were the foundation of the American form of government that promised man the dignity the Deity originally gave him and other nations sought to wrest from him. No despots, standing armies, or indolent monarchs cheated Americans of their natural rights, and they were destined to "reach a point of exultation which the proud Roman never knew and to which a son of Britain could not without presumption aspire." But if they blinded their senses with poisons, Americans could not win their fortunes, indeed they would see the Republic come to ruin.[17]

Between such appeals to reason, the young scholar wrote essays on other subjects and sent some to literary journals. Ancient history was his favorite theme. "We dwell with pleasure on the institutions of the Greeks because they first proclaimed the great principles of liberty, and of the sovereignty of the people," he told schoolboys at Aurora Academy, and added that, after all, "we Yankees also live in the midst of a barbarian world." He broke into print when Lewis Gaylord Clark, editor of the popular *Knicker-bocker*, published his essay on "Aristomenes the Messenian," the first of four articles by Morgan to appear in the journal during 1843. Relating the history of the Messenian's revolt against Sparta, he drew numerous comparisons with the American revolution, and especially between Aristomenes and George Washington, both "studded with numerous virtues but untouched by even a solitary crime." The article was well received and Clark asked for more.[18]

The comparison of the American experience to the golden age of Greece, commonly drawn in the United States, produced in western New York a virtual cult of classicism. Ever since the state's land commissioners gave classical names to the townships in the military tract, the region was inundated with such place names as Ithaca, Troy, Delphi, Hannibal, Marcellus, Brutus, Cato, and Sempronius. Its numerous turnpikes and waterways carry-

---

[17] "An Address on Temperance Pronounced at Tupper's Corners," August 2, 1842; "An Address on Temperance Delivered at Springport," May 5, 1843; "An Address on Temperance Delivered at Scipio," December 10, 1843, Morgan MSS.
[18] "Essay on the History and Genius of the Grecian Race, Delivered before Students of Aurora Academy," November 8, 1841, *ibid.*; Aquarius (pseud.), "Aristomenes the Messenian," *The Knickerbocker*, XXI (1843), 25–30.

ing traffic from the inland recalled the image of Roman splendors. Pillared porticoes were the distinctive mark of its architecture. Schoolboys and grown men belonged to fraternal orders based on Greek models like the "Order of the Gordian Knot," established by Morgan in Aurora's abandoned Masonic lodge.

The ponderous quality of the classic revival and of the temperance crusade was inherent in the stoic state of mind that fashioned them. A soaring idea perhaps occasioned by some light-headedness and a soaring archway conflicted with the image of man adhering to nature's laws. "There is a wisdom in the works of nature to which the mind yields an instinctive admiration," Morgan said in one of his lectures. Such grim yielding was inherited from Puritan theology and the austerity might never have been lost but for the grandeur of nature west of the Hudson. Through Morgan's hard temperance lectures there ran a soft and poetic stream of images about the Republic's broad plains and rolling valleys. Across the limitless realm of the philosopher's nature lay the finite boundaries of the nationalist. Before America's vast resources cold reason sometimes gave way to purple prose. When, in the spring of 1843, Morgan visited Niagara Falls, then still considered the most spectacular sight on the continent, this streak of romantic chauvinism revealed itself to the full. A few notes scribbled at the cataracts were later turned into "Thoughts at Niagara" and published in the *Knickerbocker* that autumn. The theme was the contrast between the Canadian and American falls:

Both of the same majestic pattern, equally lofty, created by the same stream and side by side; but the [Canadian] more powerful, more irresistible, more overwhelming, while the latter possesses another kind of beauty, less angry, less furious, less threatening, but yet grand and magnificent, and, take away the other fall, incomparable. . . . The Canada fall however can gain nothing by the

wearings of time. It can have no larger proportion, no higher
ledge; but on the other hand some shifting rock, some rupture in
the bed of the river above, may direct the larger share into the
American channel. . . .

Great Britain stretches her dominion through the world. The
channel of her power is deeper and its full current sweeps along
with irresistible force. She has obtained her full meridian. . . . Our
Republic in contrast, presents the figure of aspiring and expanding
youth and vigorous age.[19]

Beyond the falls lay Canada, and it was hard in the days
of "rounding out the continent" and "reaching natural
boundaries" to look across to an English possession and
not add a few metaphors to the rhetoric of manifest destiny.
Morgan was susceptive to expansionist doctrines though a
sense of national honor and political realities tempered his
enthusiasm. The critical fact was, as he wrote a friend,
that Locofoco politicians "allied most naturally with the
slave power." [20] He thought the annexation of Texas high-
way robbery by Democratic politicians bent on increasing
their strength in Congress. Expansion was less important
than internal progress, especially when the former threatened virtue.

"Thoughts at Niagara" revealed the blend of Morgan's
natural law philosophy with a type of village pantheism
that cropped up in a number of his earlier lectures. "It
would have been a bright example to the friends of democracy," he said during his talk on the Greeks, "if some
people, aided by the simple impressions of nature, had
erected a republic under which to spend their infancy as
well as maturity." The early Greeks, ruled by kings and
aristocracies, could not "escape the reproach of having

[19] "Thoughts at Niagara," *The Knickerbocker*, XXII (1843), 194-95.
[20] Morgan to William Allen, April 5, 1845, Morgan MSS, New York
Historical Society. Morgan fitted well, if unconsciously, into the "Young
America" frame of mind. See Merle Curti, "Young America," *American
Historical Review*, XXXII (1926), 34-55; also Albert K. Weinberg,
Manifest Destiny (Baltimore: Johns Hopkins Press, 1935).

bowed their heads in the attitude of slaves." That democratic political theory rested on the complex reflections
of a Locke or Jefferson rather than on simple impressions
of nature akin to his visions at Niagara did not now occur
to Morgan. He had not yet read Turgot or heard of
Auguste Comte and their view that before men thought
scientifically they were at the mercy of theology. He never
paid much attention to the history of ideas because he was
certain that since the dawn of creation men, indeed all
animals, were guided by plain reason. This postulate of a
rational history he would attempt to prove over and again
by studies in animal psychology that were climaxed by his
great book on the American beaver. Now he sent an article
to the *Knickerbocker* entitled "Mind or Instinct," in which
he sought to show that animals adjust to their environment
through thought, not instinctually as most writers claimed.
From Buffon's *Natural History*, farmers' almanacs, and
neighbors' tales he culled numerous examples illustrating the
capacity of animals to memorize, ponder, and decide. Meta-
physicians denied them a "thinking principle," he wrote,
because they forgot that man himself had progressed from
a mental level akin to that of the beasts. It was an idea taken
from Buffon and reminiscent of an observation by the
twenty-four-year-old Darwin, just ten years before, at
Fuegia. But Morgan gave it his own and distinctive shape:

The culmination of the intellectual endowments of man has
raised him to such a degree above the other orders of animated
existence, that he claims the exclusive possession of the Thinking
Principle; forgetting, while he surveys the monuments of human
intelligence, that they are but the evidence of his advancement from
the savage state; and while he remained in that primitive condition
he might be considered in fact as many degrees below his present
condition in point of mental capacity as above that of the most
sagacious animals; forgetting also that had he continued in a state
of nature, like some of the tribes of Africa and America, leaving

others to judge of his intelligence from the rude vestiges of his civilization exclusively, they could scarcely attribute to him more intelligence than they would to the beaver, or even to the ant.[21]

He wrote Lewis Gaylord Clark that the article had "heavy implications." Across the manuscript he scrawled "Is there an animal hell?" Contemporary writers, making no distinction between the soul and the mind, and regarding the soul as immortal, denied one and therefore the other to animals. Morgan denied them neither. Who was to say that a Goth or a Hun had a nicer sense of right and wrong than a tiger, he asked. The heavier implication concerned man. Morgan accepted the fixity of species and special creation according to Genesis. But the statement that civilization was removed from savagery only by time and learning was a daring one to make in the shadow of Aurora's First Presbyterian Church. He denied the savage's fall from grace, his innate sinfulness and degeneracy. Yet he was simply commenting on what any one of his neighbors might have noticed: that Jed Morgan's plow was being used by Senecas who a century before depended on the hunt; that

[21] "Mind or Instinct, An Inquiry concerning the Manifestations of Mind by the Lower Orders of Animals," *The Knickerbocker*, XXII (1843), 414. Cf. Buffon: "You unjustly compare, it may be said, an ape who is a native of the forests with a man who resides in polished society. To form a proper judgment between them, a savage man and an ape should be viewed together," quoted in Loren Eiseley, *Darwin's Century* (New York: Doubleday & Co., 1958), p. 43; Darwin, *The Descent of Man*: "Nevertheless the difference in mind between man and the higher animals, great as it is, is certainly one of degree and not of kind. We have seen that the senses and intuitions, the various emotions and faculties, such as love, memory, attention, curiosity, imitation, reason, &c., of which man boasts, may be found in an incipient, or even sometimes in a well-developed condition, in the lower animals," quoted in Bert J. Loewenberg, *Darwinism* (New York: Rinehart & Co., 1957), p. 2. See also Jay W. Fay, *American Psychology before William James* (New Brunswick: Rutgers University Press, 1939); Edwin G. Boring, "The Influence of Evolutionary Theory upon American Psychological Thought," *Evolutionary Thought in America*, ed. Stow Persons (New York: George Braziller, Inc., 1956), p. 284. "Editor's Gossip," *The Knickerbocker*, XXII (1843), 498. L. G. Clark to Morgan, October 30, 1843, Morgan MSS.

in the Aurora Academy a number of "savages" were reading Herodotus.

Morgan was not altogether pleased with this civilizing
process. His own education had not brought him very far,
and there was no progress in sight. In a way he might never
have left for Schenectady. Currently he was reading Washington Irving's *Columbus* and the "picture of primitive
society in Xaragua, with its idle and ignorant enjoyment
[was] irresistibly agreeable." As against Greeks and their
urbane abstractions, he was discovering the "aborigines'
free, sincere, unostentatious hospitality, a virtue that ob-
literates a thousand faults of civilized man and in the abodes
of wealth is seldom without the alloy of vanity, ostentation
and pride." [22] Here was a game subject for investigation.

[22] "Anacaona of St. Domingo," January, 1843, Morgan MSS.

CHAPTER II

THE BIRTH OF ETHNOLOGY

While Henry Thoreau complained that "the American has dwindled into an Odd Fellow," the Order of the Gordian Knot continued to meet regularly in Aurora's Masonic lodge. In rural areas of western New York, where rectangular land surveys put a distance between homesteads, men welcomed any means of coming together socially. Ever since the Freemasons fell into disrepute, their abandoned lodges made excellent meeting places. Secret organizations provided a sense of exclusiveness to its members, for some of whom complex rituals supplied the only color in an otherwise drab existence. In a frontier country oaths of eternal allegiance were as earnest as they were solemn. Throughout his life Lewis Morgan received and answered letters from former fraternal brothers settled in all parts of the continent.

A secret order was especially welcome to rural youths planning to establish themselves in the city. A bustling commercial center that knew men as buyers and sellers, creditors and debtors, made a new arrival from the countryside uneasy. Accustomed to the neighborly greeting, or to the electric atmosphere of a common harvest, he felt the reserve of men hurrying to fulfil their separate contracts. Wealth and progress could be as confining as the village, and the "paper aristocracy," symbol of urban oppression over the farm, was the best evidence. Visiting Geneva, a thriving banking center, Lewis Morgan gave vent to his rural contempt of the creditor soul:

The location of the domestic establishments of the citizens deserve all the praise which they have received; but the citizens as a body are reserved, distant and pernicious. There is some wealth in this place, but those who possess it live upon the interest and like all other little capitalists living in this way are the most arrogant, illiberal and narrow minded class of men in the world. Like the old woman who measures everything by the dozen eggs, the seven per cent gentry, wherever they are found, measure everything by the number of dollars from which the required sum must emanate, and as $70 is the interest on a whole thousand, to spend it is a murderous consumption.[1]

When he moved to Rochester in the late winter of 1844 and opened a law office in the heart of the business district, Morgan's fortunes grew slowly. Although the city began its recovery from six years of business depression, only a few routine and disheartening criminal cases came his way. A thief caught in the act and another found with a suitcase full of stolen goods were typical clients, he complained to a fraternal brother. Looking back, years later, he suggested that only those who have tried it could know "the real magnitude of the undertaking of young men who attempt, without advantage of business connections, and the influence of personal friends, to establish themselves in the legal profession." [2]

[1] Entry for November 21, 1845, Manuscript Journal, I, Morgan MSS. The influence of economic changes on the growth of fraternities is the theme of Georg Simmel, "The Sociology of Secrecy and Secret Societies," *American Journal of Sociology*, XI (1906), 441–98. See also A. M. Schlesinger, "Biography of a Nation of Joiners," *Paths to the Present* (New York: Macmillan Co., 1949); Alexis deTocqueville, *Democracy in America* (New York: Alfred A. Knopf, 1945), I, 106–10; N. P. Gist, "Secret Societies, A Cultural Study of Fraternalism," *University of Missouri Studies*, XV (1940), No. 4.

[2] Morgan to Ely S. Parker, August 16, 1844, Parker MSS, Library of the American Philosophical Society (hereafter cited as "Parker MSS"). Morgan to James Hall, April 10, 1845, copy in Morgan MSS, shows that he moved to Rochester between these two dates. Morgan to William Allen, February 11, 1845, February 19, 1845, Morgan MSS, New York Historical Society (hereafter cited as "NYHS"); "Memoir of Calvin Huson, Jr.," 1861, Morgan MSS.

During these years of his unemployment and apprenticeship, the order was Morgan's chief source of companionship. In Rochester he organized a branch of it among Union graduates and a few Aurora men, a process repeated by others as they left Aurora for Syracuse, Utica, Waterloo, and elsewhere. Within four years of its founding, the brotherhood had five hundred members in a dozen towns. About a third of them were Union graduates, and most were at the beginning of their careers. Communications between them grew into a mountain of letters. Once a year, at harvest time, they had a dignified and happy reunion in Aurora.

Shortly after its founding, the fraternity changed character. At a gathering in Aurora in the summer of 1843, his head filled with notions about primitive society, Morgan proposed that the order should cease to be modeled on ancient myths and copy instead the customs of the Iroquois. A fraternal order's legend must be consistent, and his proposal was put in the form of an improvement on the Gordian myth. "Gordius conceived the mighty enterprise of leading his Phrygian children to this western hemisphere, conducted them to Bhering's [sic] Strait, thence across to this western world. . . ." The Gordian Knot became "The Grand Order of the Iroquois," and made Morgan its chief, Skenandoah, named after an Iroquois friendly to Americans during the Revolution. The Aurora lodge became the Cayuga Tribe. As members moved to other cities they "found their brethren," the Mohawks, Oneidas, Onondagas, and Senecas.[3]

"Boyish qualities," as Morgan called them, ceremonies,

[3] Morgan to John Wesley Powell, September 22, 1880; Morgan to Henry Schoolcraft, February 25, 1845, *ibid*. The history of the order, in the form of its records, membership lists and communications, is preserved as part of the Morgan MSS in Rush Rhees Library. "An Address by Skenandoah . . . ," August 29, 1843, *ibid*.

rituals, and midnight excursions, dominated the order's early career. "You are aware that every association as Masons, Odd Fellows, fire and military companies, all possess uniforms," Morgan wrote, proclaiming the institution of the Oneida Tribe in Utica. "They seem to lend dignity and interest to the organizations." The "warriors" wore Iroquois costumes complete with leggings, headdress, and tomahawks at their meetings and council fires. Oratory was an important part of their gatherings, and, in speeches as in communications between them, great pleasure was derived from the use of presumably Indian figures of speech. "The tall pine in the young forest has not spoken with a forked tongue," wrote the pastor of Aurora's Presbyterian Church, a wise man of the Cayuga nation. "Our Song," composed by one of the warriors, stirred the rest:

> Then raise on high the battle cry
> We scorn the white man's laws;
> We form a band, called throughout the land
> Grand Order of the Iroquois

went its chorus.[4]

The order soon assumed a serious purpose. Imitation of Indian customs caused interest in the neighboring Iroquois, and a number of members tried to learn what they could about them. Morgan organized a "literary committee" that studied available books on Iroquois life, but these were scarce or had little of the information desired. William Stone's *Red Jacket* and *Life of Joseph Brant* had meager passages on tribal laws, and James Adair's *History of the American Indian* had even less, Morgan complained.[5] But

[4] Skenandoah, "A Proclamation . . . ," December 5, 1844; C. S. Mattoon, *et al.*, to Henry Schoolcraft, May 5, 1845, *ibid.* The song was by George B. Glendinning, adopted September 17, 1844, *ibid.*

[5] James Adair, *The History of American Indians* (London: E. & C. Dilly, 1775); William L. Stone, *The Life and Times of Red Jacket* (New York: Wiley & Putnam, 1841) and *Life of Joseph Brant* (New York: Dearborn & Co., 1838); Morgan to Schoolcraft, April 10, 1845, Morgan MSS.

the very dearth of information about the Indians inspired him to find out more about them. As a lawyer he was interested in Iroquois litigation. A romantic, he conceived the Indian past a part of the American heritage and therefore worth intensive study. "How natural and how appropriate it is for us to become interested in whatever pertains to our Indian predecessors," he told his committee.

Our fathers commenced their career on this continent with all the intelligence and improvements of the age in which they lived. They came from the midst of civilization and refinement. . . . Hence we cannot look back upon barbarous and antiquated ages during which our ancestors were slowly progressing. All our antiquities are essentially Indian.[6]

He wrote to William Stone of the need "for an order which should aim to become the vast repository of all that remains to us of the Indian . . . his antiquities, customs, eloquence, history and institutions," and envisioning a national organization, invited the historian to become an honorary member.[7] A similar letter was sent to Governor Lewis Cass of Michigan, who had published articles on the Indians of the northwest, and others were addressed to George Bancroft, Washington Irving, William Cullen Bryant, and John Quincy Adams. An enthusiastic response to his election as an honorary member came from Henry Schoolcraft, then rising to the peak of his career as an authority on Indian legends. He was impressed by the order's purposes and asked to be admitted as Alhalla, a prophet of the Iroquois.

Schoolcraft's response raised Morgan's hopes of establishing a literary society, but he was rebuffed by the majority of members, primarily interested in fraternal affairs. Embarrassed, Skenandoah wrote Alhalla that a working

[6] "An Address by Skenandoah," April 17, 1844, *ibid.*
[7] Morgan to William L. Stone, June 10, 1844, Stone MSS, NYHS.

membership could only be maintained by mixing social and intellectual functions and apologized for some of the frivolousness of the group. He asked him to address the annual council in Aurora, at which most of the "warriors" were to be present. The invitation caused some dissension between the order's "boyish" and "scholarly" factions, but the scholars won after promising the boys the usual rituals and council fires.[8]

Schoolcraft arrived in Aurora in August, 1845, and in an address that revealed the romantic and nationalist roots of American ethnology, tried to persuade the gathering of young men of the importance of Indian lore:

> Whatever may be the degree of success, which characterizes your labors, it is hoped they will bear the impress of American heads and American hearts. We have drawn our intellectual sustenance it is true, from noble fountains and crystal streams. We have all Europe for our fountainhead. . . . Nurtured as we have been from such ample sources, it is time in the course of our national development that we begin to produce something characteristic of the land that gave us birth. No people can bear a true nationality, which does not exfoliate, as it were, from its bosom, something that expresses the peculiarities of its own soil and climate . . . there must come from the broad and deep quarries of its own mountains foundation stones and columns and capitals. . . .
>
> And where, when we survey the length and breadth of the land can a more suitable element for the work be found, than is furnished by the history and antiquities and institutions of the free, bold, wild, independent native hunter race? They are relatively to us what the ancient Pict and Celt were to Britain or the Teuton, Goth and Magyar were to continental Europe. . . .[9]

[8] Morgan to Lewis Cass, August 30, 1845, Morgan MSS. See Lewis Cass, "Aboriginal Structure," *North American Review*, LI (1840), 396–433. Morgan to George Bancroft, August 16, 1844, Bancroft MSS, Massachusetts Historical Society; List of Honorary Members, November 20, 1846, Morgan MSS; Morgan to Schoolcraft, February 25, 1845, Schoolcraft MSS, Library of Congress (hereafter cited as "Schoolcraft MSS"); H. R. Schoolcraft to Morgan, March 18, 1845, Morgan MSS; Morgan to Schoolcraft, April 10, 1845, Schoolcraft MSS.

[9] The address was published by the order as *An Address Delivered before the New Confederacy of the Iroquois, August 14, 1845* (Rochester: Jerome & Bro., 1846); the quotation is from the manuscript in Morgan MSS.

It was an eloquent manifesto and recent events had given it urgency as well as a means of accomplishment. The year before, visiting in Albany, Morgan met a young Seneca browsing in a bookstore who invited him to meet some chiefs. That night, his new acquaintance acting as interpreter, Morgan interviewed several Senecas in their hotel room. He returned again the next day, and the day after, and with pencil in hand asked questions "as long as propriety would permit." [10] The tribesmen explained the organization of the Iroquois Confederacy, the structure of a tribe and clan, and supplied him with relevant Seneca terms. In this chance encounter American ethnology was born.

The young Indian was Ha-sa-ne-an-da, known to whites as Ely Parker. The son of a chief of the Tonawanda band of Senecas, he had been educated at a Baptist mission school and selected by his people to study law in order to defend them against removal beyond the Mississippi. Sixteen years old, he was attending Yates Academy in Orleans County, where his good looks broke several maiden hearts and his orations filled student halls to capacity. He spoke English perfectly and during vacations from school acted as an interpreter for Seneca delegations in Albany and Washington. Such intimacy with government officials added to the dignity and self-assurance of this boy who had been raised in a family fiercely proud of its origins and history. He learned the white man's ways, he said, only to defend his people more effectively. But he was a charming diplomat. Eventually, he served on General Grant's staff as brigadier general and wrote out the Articles of Surrender at Appomattox, where he shocked General Lee, who mistook him for a Negro.[11] Parker was in Albany with a delegation seek-

[10] "Copy of an Address . . . ," April 17, 1844, Morgan MSS.
[11] Mrs. Louis Bacheldor, "Letter to the Editor of the Buffalo Express," clipping n.d. in Parker MSS. Parker's career and character are described in Arthur C. Parker, *The Life of General Ely S. Parker* (Buffalo: Buffalo Historical Society, 1919); besides an extensive collection of his papers in

ing aid from the state in a conflict that began six years before and lasted another two decades.

After Sullivan's campaign a state commission supervised the removal of Iroquois from their lands and by 1790 forced the tribes to relinquish most of them in return for direct payments and annuities. By the Treaty of Big Tree in 1797 the federal government acknowledged and guaranteed each tribe's title to its reservation, and the tribes in turn agreed never to make claims on other lands formerly held by them. The Senecas, most westerly of the Iroquois, were settled in the vicinity of Buffalo on four reserves that included over one hundred thousand acres and some of the richest soil in the state. The value of these lands and the city of Buffalo grew together. In 1837, Seneca real estate was worth two and a half million dollars.

Among the many land speculators then active in western New York was the Ogden Company, a subsidiary of the great Holland Land Company. Its managers, Thomas Ogden of Buffalo, Joseph Fellows of Geneva, and James Wadsworth of Geneseo, supported ardently Andrew Jackson's policy of removing Indians across the Mississippi. In 1832 they persuaded Congress to purchase reservations in Wisconsin on which to settle the Senecas. But the tribesmen refused to move, holding to the Treaty of Big Tree. Agents acting as "contractors" for the Ogden Company now descended on them and distributed ten thousand dollars to chiefs willing to relinquish tribal land titles. Like the case of the Cherokees in Georgia, Seneca removal soon grew into a state and national controversy. Political factions and even churches mustered forces on either side. The Quakers aided the Indians with funds and publicity, while a group

the Library of the American Philosophical Society, there is a brief "Autobiography," in *Buffalo Historical Society Publications,* VIII (1905), 520–36. Manuscript chapters of an unfinished second biography by A. C. Parker are in the Parker MSS.

of Buffalo clergymen including Reverend John Schermerhorn gave removal their blessing. "I am confident," Schermerhorn wrote the kindly missionary Asher Wright, scold-
ing him for agitating the Indians and defending his own
investments in the Ogden Company, "that I am promoting
the best interests of the Indians and the cause of Christian
benevolence." [12]

The federal government re-entered the conflict in October, 1837, when President Van Buren commissioned Ran-
som H. Gillet, Jacksonian congressman from western New
York, to make a new treaty providing for the removal of all
Senecas to Kansas and approving the sale of their lands to
the Ogden Company for two hundred thousand dollars.
Gillet acquired signatures from forty-three of an estimated
ninety-one chiefs. But the Senate's Committee on Indian
Affairs could not recommend ratification until a majority
of a full and open council approved the treaty.

Again the Ogden Company sent agents to the reservations. The Society of Friends reported that eight chiefs
received twenty thousand dollars for their influence over
the rest. Commissioner Gillet reserved a hotel room in
Buffalo where he invited Senecas to enjoy themselves and
elect a new tribal council. He gained eight signatures more,
and by such means the treaty was finally ratified in 1840.[13]

A few Senecas emigrated, but most stayed on their lands

[12] John Schermerhorn to Asher Wright, December 7, 1837, Parker MSS.
Senate Document No. 156, 29 Cong., 2 sess., 1847, is a history of the
Seneca's case; Orlando Allen, Henry Willcox, James Stryker, and Heman
Potter to Thomas L. Ogden and Joseph Fellows, June 23, 1838, Parker
MSS, describes the agents' activities, as do the Society of Friends, *The Case
of the Seneca Indians* (Philadelphia: Merrihew & Thompson, 1840), and
Henry S. Manley, "Buying Buffalo from the Indians," *New York History*, XXVIII (1947), 313–29.
[13] Ely Parker to S. H. Cone, June 8, 1846, Parker MSS. "The Journals
of Henry A. S. Dearborn," *Buffalo Historical Society Publications*, VII
(1904), 35–225, narrate the process of treaty-making with the Senecas
from the point of view of the representative from Massachusetts at these
negotiations.

and drove off all agents, settlers, and government officials. In 1842 fresh bribes and promises persuaded a majority to relinquish the Tonawanda Reservation. None of the Tonawanda band was a party to this agreement; sacrificed without consent, they planned to have all treaties abrogated. As one part of their strategy, they sent Ely Parker to school.

These events brought the Grand Order in touch with the harsh realities of Indian life. Shortly after Morgan returned from Albany, the order elected Ely Parker an honorary member and invited him to speak in Aurora. Within a few weeks the "warriors" listened to the boy describe in fluent English the troubles of his people. The image of noble savages stalking the forest was replaced by the picture of hundreds of families driven from their farms and facing the prospect of trekking across half a continent to pitch tents on the blistered soil of Kansas. "The Order must make the Indian the object of its benevolence and protection," Morgan wrote, and to a member of the order in Geneva he declared, "We must aid him to escape the devices of Satan and all such White folk." [14] Henry Schoolcraft was told that

> The fate of the Indian races of our Republic is to some extent in the hands of the present generation of which we constitute a portion, and our National character is deeply involved in the Red man's future destiny. If therefore we can take an early stand in behalf of the Indian; encourage a generous feeling towards him; in a word stand up to vindicate his rights and watch over his political prosperity, the Order of the Iroquois will become the institution which our country needs above all others.

But exactly how to aid the Senecas? When several members of the order suggested petitions requesting the Senate to abrogate the recent treaties, Morgan rejected the pro-

[14] Morgan to Parker, May 8, 1844, Parker MSS; Morgan to Stone, June 10, 1844, Morgan MSS; Morgan to William Allen, October 29, 1845, Morgan MSS, NYHS.

posal. He was aware of the corruption that lay at the source of the treaties. But as a lawyer he appreciated the rule, long since read into the Constitution by John Marshall, that the validity of a law is not affected by the motives of its authors. The answer to removal was integration, he thought, not endless squabbles over land titles. A realistic Indian policy must begin with the assumption that the Indian "cannot hold out against the onward tide of population," and that they "must prepare to be incorporated into the great brotherhood of American nations as equal citizens; perhaps even be engrafted on our race. I sincerely hope this may be the result."

Morgan thought that education was the best means of facilitating such integration. At his suggestion, the order began a campaign to raise money for the education of individual Senecas. Ely Parker left Yates to finish his studies at the Aurora Academy, sponsored and financed by the brotherhood. "I am glad you are attending diligently to your studies," Morgan wrote him. "All eyes are upon you and if you establish a good character as a student and as a man, I have no doubt you will find something in Aurora worth having." Ely's sister Caroline and one of her friends were sent to Aurora Academy on the contributions of twenty-eight "warriors."

But Parker had not yet accepted the "onward tide." He found little in Aurora worth having. To fellow students at the academy he lectured on the tranquility of Indian life, and he threw barbs at the greed of civilized men. In March, 1846, he completed his education and left for Washington to take charge of the Senecas' campaign.[15]

Following custom, the Indians petitioned the President, the War Department, then in charge of Indian affairs, and

[15] Morgan to Schoolcraft, May 12, 1845, December 12, 1845, Morgan MSS. See *Fletcher* vs. *Peck*, 6 *Cranch* 87 (1810). A discussion of this case as it applies to Indian land controversies is in Max Lerner, "John Marshall

the Senate to help them. President Polk, sympathetic to the Senecas' cause but under the influence of his Secretary of War, William Marcy, contended that he could not go beyond the face of a treaty. He agreed to suspend its execution until the Senate re-examined it.[16]

The hearings of the Senate Committee on Indian Affairs in the spring of 1846 marked the beginning of applied anthropology in the United States. Because it became apparent that few in Washington would support abrogation, the Tonawandas decided to plead for exemption from the treaties on the grounds that they had not been a party to them and because lands worth two hundred dollars an acre were being sold for $2.50. But an additional and major contention was that the Senate, in directing that a treaty be signed by a majority of chiefs in council, deprived the tribe of its independence. The Iroquois made no laws or agreements, Parker held and Henry Schoolcraft, acting as an expert witness, testified, without the unanimous consent of all their chiefs and sachems. The majority principle was not known among the tribesmen. Schoolcraft also supplied testimony showing that prevalent methods of Indian agriculture made it impossible for the Senecas to farm in Kansas or to survive by crowding on their remaining lands in the east.[17]

The case remained in committee until the following session. In the meantime sentiment favoring emigration increased on the Tonawanda Reservation, but two-thirds of

---

and the Campaign of History," *Columbia Law Review*, XXXIX (1939), 396–438. Morgan to Parker, November 14, 1845, Parker MSS; "Petition Pledging Contributions . . . ," December, 1845, L. H. Morgan MSS, Wells College Library, Aurora, N.Y.; Parker, "Composition Read before Students at Cayuga Academy," November 18, 1845, Parker MSS.

[16] E. Parker to Morgan, March 21, 1846, Morgan MSS; Parker to S. H. Cone, June 8, 1846, Parker MSS.

[17] Parker to Schoolcraft, May 2, 1846, Schoolcraft MSS; Schoolcraft to Parker, May 7, 1846, Parker MSS; Parker to Morgan, May 5, 1846, Morgan MSS.

those who started for Kansas in the summer died along the way. As a result petitions in behalf of the Indians flooded the Senate and meetings protesting their expulsion took place in Rochester, Buffalo, and several towns between.[18]

Before Parker had left for Washington, the Grand Order of the Iroquois offered him its aid. The Tonawandas called a special council to discuss the offer, and Chief James Johnson voiced their response: "We have not craved their assistance, but they afforded it of their own free will. I cannot believe, although we have many times been deceived by the treacherous white men, that they will deceive us, if we confide in them and accept the assistance they offer." Morgan's warriors were encouraged to circulate petitions and to send delegates to Washington. Charles Porter, Morgan's future brother-in-law, took charge of the campaign. Memorials were posted in towns and villages, and one hundred were sent to Schoolcraft to be used in New York City. Members were urged to save money for a trip to the capital. The Indians had led the order from benevolence to politics.[19]

In March, 1846, several hundred persons met in the courthouse at Batavia, New York, on the call of the Grand Jury of Genesee County. A memorial in behalf of the Senecas was brought to the floor. Morgan, who appears to have had little to do with the organization of the meeting, supported it with such fervor that he was appointed to deliver the memorial to the President and to the Senate.

He left for Washington two weeks later, stopping off in

[18] Lewis Parker to Ely Parker, June 11, 1847; R. B. Warren to E. Parker, June 16, 1849, Parker MSS; E. Parker to Morgan, February 13, 1847, Morgan MSS.

[19] "Report of a Seneca Council held at . . . the Tonawanda Reservation, January 1, 2, 1846," Ely Parker translator, in L. H. Morgan, Manuscript Journals, I; Morgan to Henry Haight, December 25, 1845, Morgan MSS; Charles T. Porter to Henry Schoolcraft, January 10, 1846, Schoolcraft MSS.

Albany to urge action on Governor Silas Wright but found him "wonderfully cautious." The state had no authority in the matter, nor was it possible to "look below the face of a law," Wright insisted. Petitions, Morgan learned, had persuaded the legislature to appropriate ten thousand dollars to aid the Senecas.[20]

In New York City, Morgan visited the Navy Yard and admired Trinity Church. On the suggestion of Henry Schoolcraft, he was invited to deliver a paper on Iroquois government before the New York Historical Society. He was struck by the dignity of the society's members. Albert Gallatin presided. "It was the first time that I took my seat among them and enjoyed it much . . . the savans [*sic*] of New York were present." It was an exhilarating evening, and successful. The chairman asked him to return. In Philadelphia, Morgan carefully copied the dimensions of the Girard College building and declared it the most beautiful and majestic edifice in the nation. But the city of Washington held the greatest treasures. He visited the Patent Office, the nation's scientific center, and marveled at its exhibits. At the National Institute for the Promotion of Science, parent of the National Museum, he carefully examined "Egyptian, South American and Indian curiosities," noting that the last were pitiful. "The most interesting case in the gallery of the Institute is that which contains the original Declaration of Independence and the coat-rest and pants of Washington, worn by him in 1783." He paid a call on John Quincy Adams and listened to the old man reminisce about Benjamin Franklin. He visited the President's home and the Senate, of which "any American must be proud—Webster—Calhoun—Crittenden—make it a great

[20] "Notes of an Expedition to Washington . . . April 3 to May 4, 1846," Morgan MSS.

assembly." For one who revered the Republic, Washington was overwhelming. So much so that Morgan's journal contained no mention of the purpose of his trip or of his labors in behalf of the Indians. Presumably he delivered the Genesee memorial but, perhaps because Parker was not then in the city, he appears to have done little more.[21]

The Senate Committee on Indian Affairs made its report the following February. Having considered the allegations of fraud and misrepresentation, it held that to set aside the treaties "would not only tend to unsettle the whole of our Indian policy but would open a field of interminable difficulties, embarrassment and expense." For ten years more the Tonawandas fought their case and chased settlers from their lands. In 1857, Congress at last authorized them to buy back acreage sold to the Ogden Company and appropriated the necessary funds.

During this turmoil over Seneca removal, Morgan redoubled his efforts to preserve a record of the Iroquois' customs. Their rapidly declining fortunes gave urgency to the project, while Morgan's willingness to help them reduced their suspicions of his inquiries. "Let us then copy those human tablets on which are inscribed the closing events in the career and destiny of the Old Iroquois," he told his fraternal colleagues. The image summed up Morgan's view of ethnology; like fossils registering the structure of a dying organism, reservations would reveal the former appearance of a decaying culture. An inspired proposal, it contained the rudiments of a lifelong mission.

[21] Morgan's part in the Seneca case was subsequently exaggerated. His close associate in the order and future brother-in-law, Charles T. Porter, in a postscript to the 1901 edition of the *League of the Iroquois* (New York: Dodd, Mead & Co.), wrote that Morgan, upon arriving in Washington, persuaded senators to reject the Seneca Treaty. There is no basis to this version nor to the story that the Senecas gratefully adopted Morgan into their tribe as a reward for his services. See below.

The first tablet copied was the very lively Ely Parker. Morgan filled several notebooks with information gleaned from Parker, who steered him away from the merely sensational aspects of Indian life to its essentials. With his encouragement, Morgan and his friends visited the Onondaga, Tonawanda, and Buffalo Creek reservations and soon learned techniques of successful inquiry. "Ask simple questions," Isaac Hurd, one of the most dedicated members of the group, warned. "It will not do to ask questions and then answer them as best suits the fancy of the investigator." [22] Such prudence marked the beginning of scientific ethnology.

Henry Schoolcraft was kept in touch with his colleagues' progress and informed of all their adventures. "Three of us started in season," Morgan wrote him, reporting a visit to a council fire of the confederacy, "and spent the whole last week in attendance. . . . Learned much not known before. Their laws of descent are quite intricate. . . . They follow the female line and as children always follow the mother, and the man never is allowed to marry in his own tribe, it follows that the father and the son are never of the same tribe." Much of his future research hinged on this discovery, though for more than a decade it seemed a mere curiosity to him. At Buffalo Creek he drew up the details of the Iroquois' long house and noted, among much else, the purpose of the famous sacrifice of a white dog. "All the sins of the past year are supposed to be transferred to the animal and the new year is commenced in purity." Part of the fascination of Indian lore was its similarity to ancient custom.

[22] Skenandoah, "Proclamation . . . ," August 13, 1846; Isaac Hurd, "The Onondaga Nation," in Morgan MSS. Other writings by Morgan's associates in the collection are Outalisse (pseud.), "An Essay on Indian Remains," n.d.; George Riley, "Description of An Indian Council, October 1–3, 1845"; and William Hosmer, "Genundewah, A Legend" (1845).

As the troop of wandering scholars learned more about their subject, the essential features of ethnological study came to light. It was not history but a comparative science that must classify institutions rather than narrate events. The Iroquois appeared to have a political organization that was sane and systematic, "a fabric as beautiful as it is remarkable," Morgan concluded. He grew impatient with the prevalent romantic school of Indian literature. "How then shall a just estimate of the Iroquois be formed if we confine ourselves to their exploits upon the war-path and in council?" [23]

The Tonawanda residents grew especially receptive to questioning. Morgan helped them draw up memorials to Congress and the state legislature, a service that made his inquiries seem relevant. The older Parkers collected implements that he brought away and stored at home. But the ease with which he gained information was also a sign of demoralization among the Indians. Most of the tribesmen, believing they would soon lose their farms, ceased to care for them. Homes were ill kept and poverty widespread. Such squalor led to alcoholism and to crime. Ceremonies that once were carefully guarded from intruders took on the quality of performances.

In October, 1846, Morgan and two friends, Charles Porter and Thomas Darling, visited the Tonawanda Reservation to observe the annual corn harvest festival. While there, it occurred to them to apply for adoption into the tribe. The request was resented by some chiefs, who had to be reminded that the three white men had proved their friendship and that one had even journeyed to Washington in their behalf. After some deliberation it was decided

[23] Henry Schoolcraft, *Notes on the Iroquois* (New York: Bartlett & Wellford, 1846), pp. 284-85; Skenandoah, "A Message . . . , 1846," Morgan MSS.

to adopt the visitors, provided that they paid for the expense of food and entertainment. The honor was not given freely and the ceremony which followed made Ely Parker pensive:

As I heard the long shrill whoops and looked upon the motley group of warriors who had stripped themselves for the dance, I could not avoid reflecting upon the changed condition of the Indian race. Once the savage yell and the painted band was the terror of the white man. Men, women, and children were alike victims to the unmitigated fury of the Indian. As the dancers played their warlike antics before me, with pleasure I thought of the time when my fathers were strong, when their arms were felt over half the American continent, when with joy they danced around the captive bound for torture at the stake. The warlike features have not changed, the same spirit burns within the bosom of their children, and though now they have not a captive to torture at the stake, yet they can celebrate the adoption of their white brothers into their nation.[24]

That day and the next Morgan filled several notebooks. A Seneca warrior of the Hawk clan, he was entitled to know all but the most secret rituals. Parker acted as his interpreter and scribe and secured the likeliest informants. In the following months Morgan's knowledge grew rapidly and essays on the Iroquois began streaming from his pen.

During 1847 the Grand Order slowly disintegrated. "Warriors" acquired business interests and families that left less time and energy for the fraternity. "I have rooted the Indian out of my mind," Isaac Hurd wrote from the Auburn Theological Seminary, where he was now preparing for the ministry. Another member, Henry Haight, left for St. Louis to begin a law practice that would end when he was elected governor of California. Albert J. Myer, a "warrior" at Hobart College, graduated and started on a colorful career that eventually made him the first chief of the

[24] Entry for January 4, 1846, Manuscript Journals, I; E. Parker, "A Report of the Adventures of Lewis Morgan, Charles Porter and Thomas Darling at Tonawanda, October 31, 1846," *ibid.*

army's signal corps. Morgan stopped managing the order, now impatient with its "merriment and irrelevancy." [25]

But the experience had made Morgan the foremost Iroquois authority in the country. In the four years that followed he wrote tirelessly on the Indians. The New York Historical Society invited him to speak again, this time on Iroquois trails and monuments. George Squier asked him to draw a map of these for his own book on the subject.[26] George Hooker Colton, editor of the *American Whig Review*, the chief literary organ of the Whig party, published a series of fourteen articles by Morgan in the form of letters in honor of Albert Gallatin, then president of the New York Historical Society. Published under the pseudonym "Skenandoah," during 1847 and 1848, they were widely read, brought him a dollar and a half a page, and were reprinted by a literary journal in Pittsburgh.[27]

In the spring of 1847, Governor John Young of New York visited Hartford's Historical and Antiquarian Museum and, noting its impressive Indian collection, called on his state to build a similar one. The Regents of the University of New York made an appropriation for the project, and asked citizens to aid in "furnishing relics of the ancient masters of the soil." Morgan's response was immediate. "Such a cabinet, it is true, would contain but little to instruct," he wrote the regents, "yet it would be all it pretended—a momento of the red race . . . enabled to speak for itself through these silent memorials." He supplied the regents with the names of various collectors in the state, described the extent and quality of their wares, and began

[25] Isaac Hurd to Morgan, November 17, 1846; Skenandoah, "Report of the Committee on Literary and Social Activities, Turtle Tribe," n.d., *ibid.*
[26] *Proceedings of the New York Historical Society for 1847* (New York, 1847), n.p.; entry for May 4; E. George Squier to Morgan, March 20, 1849, Morgan MSS.
[27] *The American Whig Review*, V (1847); VI (1848), *passim. Olden Times* (Pittsburgh), I (1847); II (1848), *passim.* G. H. Colton to Morgan, September 14, 1846, Morgan MSS.

forwarding his own. Between 1848 and 1851 he sent over 250 items to Albany, some bought on reservations and others excavated at former Indian sites. His stone mortars and pestles, chisels, knives, tomahawks, kettles, necklaces, pipes, drums, musical instruments, athletic equipment, and items of Iroquois dress became the core of the New York Museum's Indian collection.

As valuable as the articles were the lengthy descriptive annotations that he inclosed. In three separate reports Morgan explained the use and history of each item he forwarded. Painfully precise, these papers were models of ethnographic reporting. Like the fourteen letters on the Iroquois, they spread Morgan's reputation as an Indian expert.[28]

Much of this was at the expense of his law practice, and Morgan often wavered between giving up one or the other occupation. During court sessions he devoted himself exclusively to litigation, trying hard to forget the Indian. Then some item would turn his attention to the Iroquois and for weeks his office remained unattended. In the spring of 1849 he applied for an appointment as sub-agent for the New York Indians, a Federal post recently vacated. The position, which paid seven hundred dollars a year, would allow him to pursue his research freely and to report the grievances of his charges, which, as he complained to Henry Schoolcraft, was never done by former agents. He asked Senator William Henry Seward of New York for aid in winning the position, but it was quickly awarded to a political favorite.[29]

[28] New York University, *Reports on the Cabinet of Natural History* (Albany), II (1848), 84–91; III (1849), 65–95; V (1851), 67–117.
[29] Morgan to E. Parker, September 26, 1848, Parker MSS; Morgan to H. R. Schoolcraft, April 28, 1849, Schoolcraft MSS; Morgan to Seward, May 4, 1849, Seward MSS, Rush Rhees Library, Rochester (hereafter cited as "Seward MSS").

In the following year Morgan resolved to bring his Indian studies to an end by publishing a definitive book on the Iroquois. Reworking his articles for the *Whig Review* and the reports to the regents, he wrote the manuscript of *The League of the Iroquois* in less than six months. A small edition was published in 1851 in Rochester and New York, and another in London.[30]

Tracing briefly three hundred years of Iroquois history gleaned mostly from English and French writers, Morgan devoted the rest of his volume to systematic accounts of life among the tribesmen. Books I and II were expanded versions of his "Letters" in the *Whig Review* that depicted the Iroquois' physical surroundings, their religion, government, ceremonies, domestic customs, and games. The third book described their economy, tools, homes, and clothing, in the manner of his reports to the New York regents, then gave some account of their languages, and ended with a discussion of the Indians' destiny. The *League* was a masterful statement of its subject. Thirty years later, John Wesley Powell, the first director of the Bureau of American Ethnology, declared it "the first scientific account of an Indian tribe given to the world." Long before then Francis Wayland called it "the most remarkable book of its kind I have ever read." Later anthropologists gained much further knowledge of the Iroquois, but generally agreed with Powell's estimate, and today Morgan's book still remains the most comprehensive single volume on the New York Indians.[31]

[30] *League of the Ho-de-no-sau-nee, or Iroquois* (Rochester: Sage & Bros., 1851; New York: H. H. Newman, 1851). The London edition by Chapman is mentioned in Margaret Butterfield's exhaustive "Lewis Henry Morgan's League of the Iroquois: A Bibliography," an unpublished paper in the Morgan Collection, Rush Rhees Library.

[31] John Wesley Powell, "Sketch of Lewis Henry Morgan," *Popular Science Monthly*, XVIII (1880), 114; Francis Wayand to Morgan, July 12, 1865, Morgan MSS; William N. Fenton, "Iroquois Studies at Mid-

The *League* initiated the objective method of ethnological research without fully acquiescing in it. Based on Morgan's observations and on facts gathered from Indian informants rather than hearsay, it avoided some of the exaggerations and misconceptions that marked earlier and subsequent portraits of the Indian.

Ever since they came to the New World, Europeans wrote accounts of its inhabitants, but none had escaped the vice of describing another culture in the lineaments of his own. Most looked on the Indian from the viewpoint of Christians and conquerors. The great body of descriptive literature produced by Jesuit and Protestant missionaries was colored by the assumption that had sent them into the wilderness, that the Indian was the devil's agent. Others commonly saw him as fallen from the grace of God, a notion underlying John Winthrop's brief commentaries on the subject as well as Henry Schoolcraft's prolific writings. The fall from grace accounted for most of the "heathen's" peculiarities, and the term generally summed up its authors' conclusions.

Another view was contained in the use of the term "savage" and usually included other than religious measures of the Indian's deficiency such as his inferior economy, his strange marriage customs, the absence of written bodies of law and of private property. Writers with a less righteous outlook explained the Indians' eccentricities by finding their sources in the ancient past. This led to the use of European political nomenclature in the description of their government, a habit that prevented observers from uncovering the true nature of Indian institutions and that Morgan, years

Century," *Proceedings of the American Philosophical Society,* XCV (1951), 296–310. Roy Harvey Pearce, *The Savages of America* (Baltimore: Johns Hopkins Press, 1953), is a detailed, critical history of Indian studies in the United States.

later, was the first to criticize effectively. Captain John Smith of the Virginia Colony, for example, was one of a long line of chroniclers to compare an Indian chief, in this case Powhatan, to an ancient emperor. James Adair was convinced American aborigines were related to the biblical Jews. Other writers traced them to the Tartars, the Spartans, the Visigoths, or any number of European nations.

Morgan's *League* was not free of such schemes and, by the standards of modern ethnology, it was in some portions a tract. But Morgan's value judgments were few and rarely put in declarative terms. He meant none of his conclusions to serve as excuses for further conquest. The purpose of the book, he wrote in its first sentence, was "to encourage a kindlier feeling towards the Indian, founded upon a truer knowledge of his civil and domestic institutions, and of his capabilities for future elevation." The sentence has a ring of benevolence, repugnant to modern ethnology. It reflected the common belief that European and American culture represented a higher stage of social life than the Indian's. That the Iroquois could be "elevated" was one part of the doctrine that marked them for destruction, a paradox Morgan recognized when he wrote that civilization is "aggressive as well as progressive." But while others justified the conquest of Indians by placing them low on the scale of human progress, Morgan thought that the Iroquois might have advanced of their own accord:

If their Indian empire had been suffered to work out its own results, it is still problematical whether the vast power they would have accumulated and the intellect which would have been developed by their diversified affairs, would not, together, have been sufficiently potent to draw the people from the hunter into the agricultural state. . . . It cannot be denied that there are some grounds for the belief that their institutions would eventually have ripened into civilization.

The intrinsic charm of Iroquois existence was a prevalent theme in the *League*. "It would be difficult to describe any political society in which there was less oppression and discontent, more of individual independence and boundless freedom," Morgan wrote. His most subjective conclusions grew from his assertion that Iroquois government could be classified according to Aristotle. Morgan cherished a belief in the progression of political institutions from the monarchical, the earliest, through the aristocratic and oligarchic to the democratic, "the last and most truly enlightened." He conceived Iroquois government to be similar to the ancient Greek oligarchies, "though there was in the Indian fabric more fixedness, more dependence upon the people, more of vigor." This led him to ascribe great wisdom to the founders of the Iroquois Confederation and to the unknown authors of their constitution, who took on the appearance of a Solon or a Cleisthenes. Francis Parkman complained about this aspect of the *League* in his review of it. "In his pages their peculiar institutions assume an appearance of too much studied adjustment and careful elaboration." The fault, Parkman thought, lay in Morgan's ignorance of other American tribes. "It leads him to regard as the peculiar distinction of the Iroquois, that which is in fact common to many other tribes." [32]

The full force of Parkman's criticism struck Morgan ten years later and made him return to ethnological inquiry. In the meantime he looked to other pursuits.

[32] Parkman, "Indian Antiquities in North America," *The Christian Examiner*, L (1851), 424. Other reviews of the *League* were in *Rochester Daily Advertiser*, February 11, 1851; *Rochester Daily Democrat*, February 11, 1851; *The Literary World*, VIII (1851), 148; *Christian Review*, XVI (1851), 629.

CHAPTER III

THE PUNDIT

One's station in society seemed unpredictable. Establish your good character as a scholar and as a man and you will find something worth having, Morgan had written to Ely Parker. The injunction was false because Parker was soon refused admission to the bar on the ground that he was not a citizen. In his own case, Morgan studied hard to be a good lawyer and tried to make his abilities known to Rochester's business community. He looked, as one visitor noted about most of the city's lawyers, like a judge. A handsome black waistcoat falling evenly from his tall frame and a ruffled shirt marked him out among shopkeepers and canal men covered with flour dust and barge soot. His reserve was accentuated by a high starched collar that locked his head and pinched red burnsides. Intense gray eyes and lips firmly pressed together added to his judicial bearing. An uncommonly high brow was his best mark of distinction among Daniel Webster's countrymen.[1]

But his work consisted of local collection cases heard in Monroe County's Court of Common Pleas and an occasional minor criminal action in the Court of Sessions. Every so often he had a chance to argue before higher state courts and dip into constitutional law, but he remained primarily a trial lawyer of no great reputation. He worked long hours, especially during court sessions, when he frequently

[1] Blake McKelvey, *Rochester the Water-Power City 1812–1854* (Cambridge, Mass.: Harvard University Press, 1954), p. 298; daguerreotype, *ca.* 1850; passport, 1858, Morgan MSS.

spent whole nights, and days following, at his desk preparing an argument. During trials, lacking court stenographers, he was required to take down every word of a witness. The worst of it was the abuse that awaited a college-bred novice at the hands of a seasoned opponent. Personal insults, gross calumnies, and blackguardism were not uncommon in such instances, a Rochester attorney recalled years later. Because it was still considered the right of counsel to argue a point of law, a judge would rarely call him to order. If reproved, a lawyer answered that he had the right to argue his case in his own way and continued to harangue his victim. Morgan despised such coarseness and, after a time, as some of his acquaintances noted, he did not devote himself assiduously to his profession.[2]

His reputation was established by a book whose writing he always considered something of an accident. The *League of the Iroquois* received excellent notices in Rochester's newspapers and elsewhere. Morgan was invited frequently to lecture, and Rochester's Third Ward, in full bloom at mid-century, graciously opened its doors to him. Here, on quiet oak-lined streets, lived the city's merchants, bankers, lawyers, judges, and councilmen, fashioning as distinct a society as that of Back Bay or Murray Hill. Among its lions were Selah Mathews and Frederick Whittlesey, its foremost attorneys; Judge Moses Chapin; the vast Ely clan of millers; real estate men like the Reynolds and Schermerhorns; tradesmen like Jacob Gould and Edwin Scrantom.

[2] G. Danforth and L. Morgan, "Justices Court Register, 1851"; B. Davis Noxon to Morgan, March 31, 1853; Samuel Allen to Morgan, May 27, 1854, Morgan MSS. *Ely* vs. *Ehle*, 3 N.Y. 506, is a case argued and won by Morgan before the New York State Supreme Court. George H. Humphrey, "Changes in Practice of the Law in Rochester" (1892), reprinted in *RHSP*, IV (1925), 203-11; Charles Dewey, "Sketch of the Life of Lewis Henry Morgan with Personal Reminiscences," *RHSP*, II (1923), 30.

Some, like Jonathan Child, the first Mayor, built themselves vast pillared mansions and imported crystal chandeliers to swing from thirty-foot ceilings. Others lived in colonial simplicity and relied on the Erie Canal, which carried most of the Ward's capital as it swung around it, to act as a moat between their homes and the city's marketplaces.[3]

The young author was a most eligible bachelor, and among frequent invitations from the Ward's matrons he found an occasional message from one of their daughters with such declamations as "Thy thoughts are haunting me!" But for the neighborhood belles there was no satisfaction. Lewis remained distant to them, partly because such distances were not easily reduced by a gentleman. Dinners, parties, and even masquerades were staid affairs. A host risked the pastor's wrath if he allowed young couples to dance, and a hostess rarely let her daughter out of sight in the presence of a suitor. A shy nature might never overcome these barriers. Morgan had few if any romantic attachments but does not appear to have been concerned. The meetings of the Grand Order had occasionally wavered from their high purposes and ended in visits to establishments that catered to young men in particular distress. "What poor devils we all are," Morgan wrote a friend describing one such adventure and his own temptations. "Still I came away without being much disturbed; such matters are growing stale with me."[4]

[3] Virginia Jeffrey Smith, "Reminiscences of the Third Ward," *Rochester History*, VIII, No. 2 (April, 1946); the most affectionate portrait of the Ward is Charles M. Robinson, *Third Ward Traits* (Rochester: Genesee Press, 1899). Also Charles F. Pond, "History of the Third Ward," *RHSP*, I (1922), pp. 71–81.

[4] Valentine, unsigned, February 14, 1848, Morgan MSS; Morgan to William Allen, March 21, 1845, a letter in the possession of Dr. Charles Willmarth, Geneva, New York, and reprinted in *Archaeological Society of*

His practice and the state's Indian collection sometimes called him to Albany, where he visited with Uncle Lemuel Steele's family. Lemuel had left Hartford for Albany in 1816 and started out there as a paper hanger. Soon he was a Democratic alderman and chief engineer of the fire department. Eventually a power among the city's Jacksonians, he was appointed director of the Mechanic's and Farmer's Bank of Albany. His son George was Morgan's childhood friend, and the two had contemplated a European tour together. But now cousin Mary Elisabeth drew Lewis to the Steele household. She was a serious and intellectual woman, a year younger than he, and like her brother William who was about to leave for Borneo, she planned to be a missionary. Morgan liked her scholarly interests, and they talked easily about his Indian studies, or geology, law, and most matters except religion. They grew fond of their conversations and, after a time, of each other. Her valentines were as warm as any:

> Call me fond names Lewis! call me thine own!
> Speak to me always in love's low tone!
> Let not thy look nor thy voice grow cold;
> Let fond worship thy being enfold;
> Love me forever—and love me alone!
> Call me fond names Lewis! call me *thine own!*

Morgan tried to sway her from her missionary zeal, but Mary was deeply committed and certain of her Christian duties. Disappointed and gloomy, he wrote a will in May, 1851, and allotted her his copy of *The Natural History of the State of New York*, a gold chain, a silver cross, a pair

---

Central New York Bulletin, X (1955), No. 2. Parker's sister Caroline wrote a suggestive letter to Morgan years later: "Mr. Hathaway told us that when he was very young he fell in *love* with a beautiful Indian girl and he thinks that is why he is so interested in writing about Indians. I *wonder* if others that writes [*sic*] on Indian subjects ever did the same, well! Not one in ten would be as honest as Mr. H. to tell of it," C. G. Mt. Pleasant to Morgan, November 24, 1876, Morgan MSS.

of moccasins, and his Bible, "as slight evidence of my re-
memberance." [5]

But she changed her mind, decided to make Lewis her mission, and three months later they were married. They
bought a Greek style row house on Fitzhugh Street, the
Third Ward's main artery. The house was not in a style
popular in the Ward, and Chancellor Whittlesey's classic
mansion across the way emphasized its modesty. Though
they could soon afford something better, the Morgans never
moved. Morgan spent large sums of money on mahogany
furniture and decorations, and overcame his scorn for gam-
bling to purchase an occasional lottery ticket for an acces-
sory, like a bust of Hamilton for the hallway. Eventually
the house became famous for the addition of a great library
paneled with oak imported from Michigan and its book
cases carved by Morgan's skilled hands.[6]

At the end of two years of marriage the first child was
born, mentally defective. Lemuel outlived both his parents
but was not able to care for himself. A good-natured and
likable boy, he grew in the affection of his parents. A
daughter, Mary Elisabeth, was born in December, 1856,
and another, Helen King, in the summer of 1860.

The influence of Mrs. Morgan, a growing family, and a
literary reputation produced marked changes in Morgan's
life. Though he kept in touch with old friends, securing a
job for Ely Parker on the Genesee Canal Commission and
helping Ely's brother through school, the Grand Order

[5] Daniel S. Durrie, *The Steele Family: A Genealogical History* (Albany:
Munsell & Rowland, 1859), p. 23; valentine, signed Mary, February 12,
1850; "Last Will and Testament," May 30 1851, Morgan MSS. Mrs. Morgan is described in "Interview with Mrs. Millicent B. Alling, February 3,
1936," notes made by Bernhard Stern, in the possession of Mrs. Stern,
New York City.

[6] Morgan to George B. Steele, February 10, 1864, Morgan MSS. Third
Ward architecture is described by Walter H. Cassebeer, "Architecture in
Rochester," *RHSP*, XI (1932), 261–98. S. P. Ely to Morgan, January 6,
1880, Morgan MSS.

became a memory of a youthful and somewhat embarrassing
adventure. Now his chief associations were in the Ward,
and some, as with Hervey Ely, owner of the city's largest
flour mills, grew lucrative. A partnership with George
Danforth, a former classmate and an able attorney headed
for an appointment to the state Court of Appeals, enlarged
his practice. In drawing rooms and editorial offices he
traded political views with gentlemen. Against his will, he
became involved in church affairs.

Mrs. Morgan attended services regularly at the First
Presbyterian Church of Rochester, where she was sometimes accompanied by her husband. The steepled, white
stone edifice facing on Fitzhugh Street and backing on the
canal had the appearance of a fortress, and it was a fortress
of a kind. Warm winds of Unitarian and transcendental
doctrine blew vainly against its sturdy orthodoxy. Its pas-
tors were thorough men like Tryon Edwards, grandson of
one and great-grandson of another Jonathan Edwards.
"Times when error abound," Tryon noted in ancestral
fashion the year Morgan arrived in the city, "All shd. take
heed, error is subtle." Its covenant held communicants to
hard doctrine. "You believe that God has foreordained
whatsoever comes to pass, that by Adam's fall all his
posterity are born wholly depraved and they are justly
liable to endless punishment." Members were frequently
reminded that betting on presidential elections, traveling
on Sundays, or dancing were not part of Christian conduct
and that repeated violations would bring trial and excom-
munication.[7]

Mary was a devout communicant, but to her sorrow, and
to the grief of Reverend Joshua McIlvaine, who assumed the

[7] Charles M. Robinson, *First Church Chronicles, 1815–1915* (Rochester:
The Craftsman Press, 1915), p. 100; O. J. Price, "One Hundred Years of
Protestantism in Rochester," *RHSP*, XII (1933), 274–304.

ministry of the First Church in 1848, her husband never sufficiently rid himself of doubts for a public confession of his faith. For thirty years McIlvaine, who became his closest friend, tried to persuade him to confess in Christ, but Morgan remained reticent. "You are so abominably closed mouthed upon the subject even to your best friends, (which is a great fault)," the pastor wrote him years later, "take care of your soul!" To all the minister's exhortations Morgan replied only that "my heart is with the Christian religion." [8]

But his mind was not, entirely. "The mind is by nature full of religious tendencies," he wrote in the *League*. "Man when left to the guidance of his own inward passions searches after the Author of his being and seeks to comprehend the purposes of his existence, and his final destiny." He gave no ground to inward passions and therefore had none to spare towards a personal conversion. Through these years Morgan enlarged his notes on animal psychology, seeking to show that all species, including the human, receive immediate guidance from nature, and any "inner principle as implied in the term instinct" was only "a system of philosophy in a definition, an installation of the supernatural which silences at once all inquiry into the facts." [9]

He was a deist, ready to affirm that "this world and its inhabitants came into existence by the direct intervention of God, but to the question at what time, in what manner and under what circumstances, neither science nor history can yet return an answer." Someday, presumably, they could. In the meantime he concerned himself with sub-

[8] J. McIlvaine to Morgan, January 26, 1874, October 19, 1875, Morgan MSS; McIlvaine, "The Life and Works of Lewis Morgan: An Address at his Funeral," reprinted in *RHSP*, II (1923), 58.
[9] *League of the Iroquois*, p. 141; Charles E. Robinson to Morgan, n.d.; "Animal Psychology, April 7, 1857," Morgan MSS.

ordinate questions, as he called them, the answers to which
were to be found outside the portals of the First Church.
He accompanied Mary to services and avoided open controversy in order to spare her feelings. But at times he
allowed himself some act of insurgence against the cloth,
as when he disowned a nephew for becoming an Epis-
copalian minister, or when he refused to associate with
Rochester's high church clergy. Occasionally he shocked
polite company with a diatribe against the Roman Catholic
hierarchy.[10]

Morgan presented his ideas on the subordinate questions
before a number of forums in the city. He delivered the
most successful of his public lectures, entitled *Diffusion
against Centralization*, before Rochester's Athenaeum and
Mechanic's Institute in January, 1852.[11] Its theme, in part
derived from his image of the Iroquois and in part from the
rejection of the doctrines of original sin and predestina-
tion, was that inequality among men was social and arti-
ficial, rather than innate. He pictured the ideal society as
homogeneous and free of all permanent divisions according
to religion, education, ownership of property, or advantages in commercial enterprise. By all standards but one,
America achieved this ideal. "Strike out slavery, that Russian institution, and our country is paradise regained."

Two antagonistic principles, potent enough to control
man's destiny, were forever arrayed against one another.
One, centralization, dominated Europe where power,

---

[10] "Agassiz and the Theory of the Diverse Origins of the Human Race,"
a paper read before the club, May 16, 1859; John Pomeroy to Morgan,
n.d. (*ca.* 1855), Morgan MSS.

[11] *Diffusion against Centralization* (Rochester: Dewey & Co., 1852), pub-
lished at the request of the Athenaeum's directors. Theodore Parker,
Wendell Phillips, Henry Ward Beecher, and Ralph Waldo Emerson
were among the lecturers at the Athenaeum during these years. G. C.
Hoke, "History of the Rochester Athenaeum and Mechanic's Institute,"
RHSP, XIV (1936), 213–16.

Lewis Henry Morgan, from a daguerreotype in the front cover of Mrs. Morgan's copy of *The League of the Iroquois*, about 1851

Morgan about 1870–75, from a photograph presented to Millicent B. Alling

The library of the Morgan home in Rochester

Morgan the year before his death in 1881

respectability, wealth, and education were controlled by the few; the other, diffusion, characterized American life. These principles were embedded in a nation's "primary institutions," by which Morgan meant its fundamental laws or its constitution. A republican form of government, religious toleration and the separation of church and state, taxation by consent, freedom of speech, and the absence of a hereditary nobility secured diffusion. In turn these institutions could be upheld by succeeding generations

no longer than the ideas from which they spring retain their original vitality and sanction. If they survive the beliefs in which they originated, they must either be purified or fall to pieces unless they are upheld by the arm of power. But there is a vast undercurrent of society moving along with irresistible power, and with an eternal flow which is destined to swallow up all things arrayed against it. This current is the unwritten thoughts of the people . . . imbibed from surrounding influences . . . they are neither books nor constitutions, nor statute laws, they are written in the bosom of humanity.

The dialectic in Morgan's thought was evident throughout the lecture. It stemmed in part from Guizot's view that the middle classes everywhere opposed aristocracy and "fought the great battles of liberty, both in the parliament and in the field." It also reflected recent events in Rochester, where machine shops, paper mills, furniture and clothing factories introduced the city to conflicts between capital and labor.

Capital and labor are two independent powers, bound together by natural ties, but usually standing in opposite ranks. Capital is very apt to encroach upon labor, and to seize every opportunity to dictate to labor its terms. Capital has sharp perceptions and thrifty cunning while labor is unsuspecting and frequently in necessity. . . . Capital can rest when labor must be busy; it can contrive when labor is much too occupied to think; it lives in abundance when labor is often writhing in destitution. As the world has been governed, it is not surprising that capital has always gained the victory, and held labor in its servitude.

But the chief training ground for a dialectician was the sectional controversy. Since the annexation of Texas, which he regarded as a gross violation of northern political interests, Morgan feared the coming of civil war. "Still if war comes the damned abolitionists ought to be enlisted to a man," he had written a friend, because they, too, caused disunion. Morgan never associated with Frederick Douglass, who lived within a few minutes walk, or any other of the city's militant abolitionists like Susan B. Anthony and William H. Channing. For a time he supported the idea of paid emancipation proposed by his former mentor, Eliphalet Nott, who eventually became head of the New York Compensation Society. But the greater influence on Morgan was Senator William Henry Seward. When this conservative Whig lawyer threatened slavery with a higher law than the Constitution, during the Great Debate of 1850, Morgan thought the speech a marvelous achievement. "The body of the Whig party, a large section of the unsophisticated Loco-focos, together with the whole crew of abolitionists stand ready to defend your views as their own," he wrote Seward. He changed his mind about the danger of Civil War because, as he told the Senator, "you alluded in your speech to one great truth which I have often thought upon, that the laws of trade bind us together with firmer links than any political institution of our own creating ever could." The Mississippi and its tributaries, he thought, would preserve the Union against disruption by even the most fundamental of controversies. This notion, and Sewards' leadership, made him impatient with Whig attempts to placate the South. In the same year as he delivered his address on diffusion, he confided to Seward the hope that a sectional party would soon emerge to rule the country according to true democratic principles.[12]

[12] Morgan to William Allen, March 4, 1845, Morgan MSS, NYHS;

To his audience at the Athenaeum he said much the same thing, emphasizing that he was not advocating war nor, in reference to the labor question, "any arbitrary division of property or any agrarian doctrine." A democratic society and a plentiful economy could avoid class antagonisms since "the paramount safeguard of labor is the diffusion of property." Much depended upon the continuing expansion of commerce and the opening of new fields of enterprise. He was pleased to note that the trade of the world already lay in our grasp though he saw some danger that we might surpass England as marauders and become the world's chief freebooters.

Politicians and newspapermen in Rochester considered Morgan "a Whig of the most deserving sort." His suspicion of class strife was a part of Whig doctrine and one reason for his antagonism to what he preferred to call Locofoco disorder. He agreed with all good Whigs that the nation must be run by the able not the merely self-interested because, as he put it, "democracy is a principle and not an accident." When he lost the appointment to the Indian Agency in 1849, he bitterly complained that office seeking had become a business and he warned his party of giving in to the spoils system. A related threat to the homogeneous society and to good government grew from the large number of foreign born that crowded the nation's cities. During these peak years of immigration Rochester's "Dublin," as the Irish ward was called, and the German quarters of the city housed almost half of its population, strengthening the local Democratic machine. Morgan did not join the Nativist party, which was small and ineffective in Rochester, but he was in sympathy with its program. "By dispensing with all qualifications save that of temporary resi-

Morgan to W. H. Seward, February 2, 1850, March 21, 1850, May 14, 1852, December 11, 1852, Seward MSS.

dence, we have lessened the dignity of the franchise itself," he declared, and asked whether it was just to naturalize aliens who could not read and write. "A man so low in the scale of intelligence as to be without these means of improvement and so stolid as to be unwilling to acquire them, is poorly qualified to exercise in the national sovereignty." [13]

While the growth of trade insured economic equality, the diffusion of education broadened political democracy. Knowledge unfettered the mind, made a free man of a vassal, Morgan concluded at the Athenaeum and Mechanic's Institute. The lecture itself was one of several attempts to educate the citizenry in political matters. In the same year he was awarded an honorary degree by the newly established University of Rochester for serving as its attorney during the drawn-out process of gaining a charter from the state regents. As current secretary of a citizen's committee for the founding of a female counterpart to the men's college, a venture that failed for lack of support, Morgan gained great interest in female education. Eventually he took part in the establishment of Wells College in Aurora, and willed his entire estate to the University of Rochester for the advancement of higher education of women.[14]

Centralization and diffusion were apt terms to describe Rochester's economic situation at mid-century. The city's status as the "young lion of the west," the commercial gateway to the inland regions, and the flour center of America drew to a close. Buffalo, Cleveland, Detroit, and Chicago were replacing it as focal points of western commerce. The

[13] Copy of Alexander Mann to Thomas Ewing, May 2, 1849; copy of Morgan to Thomas Ewing, May 15, 1849, Morgan MSS; "Athenian Democracy," *The New York Quarterly*, III (1853), 341–42; Blake McKelvey, "Rochester: Political Trends, a Historical Review," *Rochester History*, XIV (April, 1952).

[14] Jesse L. Rosenberger, *Rochester: The Making of a University* (Rochester: University of Rochester Press, 1927), p. 22; "Barleywood Female Seminary, Volume of Records," 1852, Morgan MSS.

Genessee Valley, which fed the lake port with grain, hides, and lumber, suffered from the competition of new regions, and the flour mills of Oswego and St. Louis were supplanting those of Rochester. The merger of rail lines between Albany and Buffalo into the New York Central in 1853, profitable though it was to Rochester capitalists who built the Tonawanda and Auburn section, signaled the supplanting of local by eastern control. Morgan's fear of centralization in wealth or "respectability"—status was not yet a current term—was common among Rochester businessmen. Some were wedded to the idea of drawing profits out of commerce, or out of the earth, and declined to invest in local factories. "Mining for precious metals is really the only business which a man of sensibility ought to do," one of them wrote Morgan years later. "He stands and falls on the merits of his own enterprise, interferes with no one, and not anyone with him." The west was a safety valve for such spirits. At the Athenaeum, Morgan expressed this view:

The highest test of our republican institutions has not yet come. Can they rule and restrain a dense population? The tendency to spread abroad and occupy the vacant west has hitherto furnished a vent for our surplus population; but when this outlet is closed, and migrations cease, new social evils will arise, from which we are at present exempt. A dense population is full of grievances which a sparse one escapes.

A few Rochester capitalists migrated. Henry O'Reilly, among other things the city's first historian, together with Heman Ely, Jonathan Child, and Levi Ward, financed telegraph lines in the Great Lakes region west of Buffalo.[15] Then, in 1851, Heman Ely, a civil engineer in a family of

[15] S. P. Ely to Morgan, July 28, 1879, Morgan MSS; McKelvey, *Rochester the Water-Power City*, pp. 322–34. A history of the O'Reilly venture is preserved in the O'Reilly MSS, NYHS. O'Reilly was a leader of Rochester's anti-monopoly movement directed primarily against the New York Central. See Lee Benson, *Merchants, Farmers and Railroads* (Cambridge, Mass.: Harvard University Press, 1955), pp. 18–22, and below, chap. vi.

flour millers, discovered the advantages of building a railroad in the upper peninsula of Michigan. Since 1820, when Henry Rowe Schoolcraft served as a mineralogist on General Lewis Cass's expedition to the upper Mississippi, during which both men discovered the fascination of Indian lore, the peninsula's mineral deposits attracted attention. Later, geologists like William Keating and Douglass Houghton explored its great wealth. Since 1845, when John Burt, a surveyor, found a vast iron mountain there, the upper peninsula was the scene of brisk activity. Detroit, Cleveland, and Boston capitalists started mining operations that grew rapidly. But they faced a major problem in transporting the ore to ports on Lakes Superior or Michigan. Heman Ely, together with Rochester's Jonathan Child, Alvah Strong, and others, organized the Green Bay and Lake Superior Rail Road and during 1852 supervised the construction of a twelve-mile line from Marquette on Lake Superior to the mouth of a mine owned by Michigan capital. Within a few months the venture failed for lack of funds.

In the four years that followed, the Rochester group expanded its projects for the peninsula. It purchased one-half of John Burt's fabulous Iron Mountain, just west of Marquette, and in 1855 formed the Lake Superior Iron Company to mine and smelt the ore. In the same year it founded the Iron Mountain Rail Road Company to transport the ore to Marquette. Among two dozen Rochester men investing in the latter company was Lewis Morgan, who risked one hundred dollars and was elected one of five directors.[16] In that capacity, in July, 1855, he started on the first of many trips to Marquette.

The journey, made with a group of associates, lasted

[16] Copy of M. E. Everett to C. I. Walker, November 14, 1857, Morgan MSS. Saul Benison's exhaustive "Railroads, Land and Iron: A Phase in the Career of Lewis Henry Morgan" Ph.D. diss., Columbia University, 1953) uncovered Morgan's entrepreneurial career.

eight days. The party arrived in Toronto by steamer, then crossed Ontario on rails to Collingwood on Georgian Bay. From there a vessel took them into Lake Huron and through the newly opened canal at Sault Ste Marie, into Superior and to Marquette.

It was a breath-taking introduction to the west. The expanse of forests and lakes filled Morgan with wonder and reminded him of younger days. "There is a familiar look to this distant shore of Lake Superior for which I have not found compensation to this day in Rochester," he wrote wistfully in his journal by the moon's light. He marveled at railroad tracks thrown across the wilderness and farms in country where a few years before forests sheltered Indians. The new canal at Sault Ste Maric was a prime example of American ingenuity opening a vast continent to commerce. Marquette, a village of five hundred persons, would, he predicted, be a great city within a short time.

Heman Ely showed the visitors the peninsula's copper and iron mines on daily trips into the countryside. Morgan collected samples of ore, measured roadbeds, descended into the pits, and interviewed laborers, carefully noting their wages. His faith in the Rochester operation was complete. "The amount of ore is vast beyond all estimation . . . would stagger the belief of anyone who had not seen it. . . . The Elys must become very rich when it begins to be carried on the railway to the lake." [17] Between surveys of the company's property he hunted for partridge, caught trout, and took testimony in the preparation of suits over land claims against competitors.

The mining and carrying of wealth out of the upper peninsula of Michigan illustrated how science guided the expansion of trade and, through it, relieved centralization of

[17] "Notes of a Visit to Marquette . . . July and August, 1855," Morgan **MSS.**

capital. Surveyors and geologists uncovered mineral deposits, mining engineers brought them to the surface, civil engineers constructed railroad lines. For Morgan, science, commerce, and democracy formed an inseparable trinity. He kept abreast of geographic expeditions and scientific news of every kind. Lieutenant William Herndon's exploration of the Amazon Valley, sponsored by the navy, led him to write a lengthy description of the Andes, based on Herndon's report. "They are worth a thorough scientific expedition," he thought, "not a mere transit over them by a traveller like Humboldt." He studied volumes of Alexander Dallas Bache's Coast Survey and badgered federal officials for reports on the Pacific railroad, Perry's expedition to Japan, and the foreign commercial relations of the United States.[18]

Such interests were not unique in Rochester. The city was in the midst of a scientific renaissance at whose focal point stood the new University of Rochester, its charter providing for a non-sectarian school and the teaching of all branches of science and learning. A whole generation of the city's schoolboys were reared to a taste for science by Chester Dewey, a hard-bitten Yankee preacher with a thorough knowledge of botany, mineralogy, and chemistry. For thirty years before he taught at the university, Dewey had inspired Rochester Seminary students, one of whom later said that Dewey was "worth fifty of modern professors of chemistry and natural philosophy." His prize pupil, Henry A. Ward, developed a passion for collecting

[18] Morgan to W. H. Seward, November 17, 1854, Seward MSS; "The Andes," December 19, 1854; Joseph Henry to Morgan, June 12, 1854; copy of Morgan to Spencer Baird, September 16, 1855; Morgan to Edwin B. Morgan, February 2, 1850, Morgan MSS; Morgan to Seward, December 11, 1852, Seward MSS; Copy of Morgan to William L. Marcy, March 15, 1855; Hamilton Fish to Morgan, April 25, 1853, Morgan MSS.

mineral and zoölogical specimens and eventually made a fortune as a supplier of museum collections.

Visiting naturalists were welcomed in the city. In 1854, Louis Agassiz' widely advertised lectures filled the Athenaeum and Mechanic's Institute to overflowing. Henry Ward took the eminent man on a tour of the Genesee Gorge, impressed him with his knowledge, and was invited to Harvard to work in Agassiz' laboratory. In the following year, Benjamin Silliman gave a series of lectures in geology that were so well attended, the Athenaeum continued to offer annual courses in similar subjects and built a sizable scientific library.[19]

On a summer night in 1854, Morgan invited a number of neighbors and university men to his home and proposed the organization of a club devoted to scholarly pursuits. The suggestion received an enthusiastic response and the club met regularly, usually at his home, each month for the next twenty-five years. It is still meeting, though in a different form. Its first members were Martin Anderson, president of the university, Reverend McIlvaine, Chester Dewey, Judge Harvey Humphrey, the university's John Raymond, professor of history, E. Peshine Smith, professor of political economy, and Ashael Kendrick, professor of classics. William Watson Ely and Edward Mott Moore, the city's leading physicians, were among the early additions to its membership, kept small in order to facilitate discussions. The club included Rochester's best intellects and its meetings were soon regarded with awe as well as some derision. A few Third Warders referred to it as the

[19] John N. Pomeroy to Morgan, July 10, 1879, Morgan MSS; Blake Mc-Kelvey, "When Science Was on Trial in Rochester," *Rochester History*, VIII (October, 1946), 2; Roswell Ward, *Henry A. Ward*, RHSP, XXIV (Rochester, 1948), 27–28, 30–31; Dirk J. Struik, *Yankee Science in the Making* (Boston: Little, Brown & Co., 1948), p. 177.

Pundit Club, a name that came into general use and was eventually adopted by the members.[20]

Pundits though they were, they pursued their studies seriously and with vigor. Out of respect for his position, Martin Anderson was elected chairman. The venerable Chester Dewey was its most authoritative voice. But Morgan, appointed the club's secretary, grew to be its guiding spirit and assumed direction of its discussions. "His unflagging enthusiasm permeated the whole membership," a member recalled years later, "and his rule though rigid, was salutary and even necessary." Morgan's spirited leadership helped keep together a group whose scope of inquiry knew no bounds. Martin Anderson's thirty-seven papers presented over thirty-three years included "The Origin and Dispersion of the Celtic Races," "Trial by Jury," "Arabic Metaphysics," and "The English University System." McIlvaine read papers on "The Limitations of Logic," "Sanscrit Grammar and Language," and "Comparative Philology and its Relation to Ethnology." Professor Peshine Smith discussed currency and banking problems, while Judge Humphrey read his translations of Lucretius and papers on English cathedral architecture. Chancellor Frederick Whittlesey dealt with Roman law and the United States Foreign Service.

But a common bond also held these intellects together. They shared the assumption that a whole man takes the whole of human learning for his province. Knowledge should not be kept in exclusive spheres, and while some knew more about specific topics, no subject was too foreign for the rest.

Their goal was to find man's place in a world full of

[20] "Origin and History of the Club," read before the club, October 5, 1855, Morgan MSS; William C. Morey, "Reminiscences of the Pundit Club," *RHSP*, II (1923), 99–126.

change and new discoveries. Dr. Anderson read an essay on "The Difficulty of Locating Man in the Zoological System," a subject that had transcendent implications. Cuvier's classifications presented few difficulties twenty years earlier, but his system now strained in the light of fresh discoveries. The Club followed Louis Agassiz' attempts to account for newly found biological variations and tested his theory of separate spheres of creation. McIlvaine rejected it after examining it in terms of linguistic knowledge. Dr. Moore proposed to disprove it by the use of blood samples from different regions of the world, and Morgan decided to apply ethnological data as a test. A crucial problem, it involved religious doctrines and even affected the slavery controversy. Agassiz' system seemed to justify slavery by establishing the Negro as a separate species, while the notion of a single center of creation emphasized the injustice of human servitude.[21] There was some timeliness in most of the Club's discussions. It examined free-trade theory in the light of tariff revenues and the receipts of canal commissions. Lyell's geological system was employed to study the structure of the Genesee Gorge, and the Club's lawyers compared and contrasted Blackstone and Coke with current litigation on Court House Square.

[21] During the debate in Congress over the Compromise of 1850, Morgan expressed the not uncommon sentiment of Negrophobia, based partially on the belief that the Negro was a separate species. He urged Seward to limit the expansion of slavery because "it is time to fix some limits to the reproduction of this black race among us. It is limited in the north by the traits of the whites. The black population has no independent vitality among us. In the south while the blacks are property, there can be no assignable limit to their reproduction. It is too thin a race intellectually to be fit to propagate and I am perfectly satisfied from reflection that the feeling towards this race is one of hostility throughout the north. We have no respect for them whatever." (Morgan to Seward, February 2, 1850, Seward MSS.) But in 1857, in his paper on Agassiz he wrote, "The idea of many pairs at creation, as a means of accounting for the present difference among men is, as it seems to me, an absurdity."

The Pundits resembled the American Scholar of Emerson's prescription. Familiar with their well-stocked libraries, they chose to engage and study nature, fearless of breaking down hallowed beliefs. Logic has its limitations, McIlvaine warned them, and they tuned their discussions to that proposition. Drawing vigor from raw facts of science, they tried to master them until the rapid increase of knowledge made their quest unrealistic. In 1860, therefore, the Club laid plans to found an academy of science in Rochester, but the war interrupted the enterprise. They met again after the war, then to probe the theories of Darwin and Herbert Spencer, as well as to consider the increasingly impressive research of their own Lewis Morgan. By then the Club's reputation had grown beyond the city's limits. "There is a good deal of good thinking being done in Rochester," wrote Andrew D. White of Cornell. "They have the best social club for discussing literary, political and scientific questions that I know of in the United States." "The only club to be compared with it is the Literary Club of Boston, where Lowell sits at one end and Longfellow at the other," thought Robert Carter of *Appleton's*. For many of the Pundits the association became more than an intellectual experience. Around it, wrote one, "cluster most of the tenderest and dearest recollections of my life." [22]

[22] Morgan, "Discussion of the Feasibility of Organizing a Rochester Academy of Sciences," March 27, 1860, Morgan MSS; A. D. White to David A. Wells, October 31, 1882, Wells MSS, New York Public Library; Robert Carter to Morgan, December 3, 1874; Isaac Hills to Morgan, July 3, 1872, Morgan MSS. Similar sentiments were expressed by A. H. Mixer to Morgan, February 17, 1862, Morgan MSS and Charles Pomeroy to Rossiter Johnson, October 6, 1888, Johnson MSS, New York Public Library.

CHAPTER IV

FORMS OF UNITY AND DISCORD

Years later, across the wreckage of war and the complexities of another time, the Pundits looked back fondly on their first meetings in "the little house on Fitzhugh Street." They had seemed to be at the threshold of the secrets of the universe and a science of society. E. Peshine Smith, the economist among them, introduced his *Manual of Political Economy* as an attempt to construct a skeleton of the subject "upon the basis of purely physical laws, and thus to obtain for its conclusions that absolute certainty which belongs to the positive sciences." Such confidence was the wellspring of their energy and of the joy they derived from scholarship. Its source lay in the belief that the proper subject of their study was man, not men as southerners and northerners, Republicans and Democrats, slaves and planters. In science as in politics they were Whigs, resisting the break up of a homogeneous society. Defending his view of political economy, Peshine Smith referred to statistics of life expectancy, marriage, suicide, and crime rates which showed such widespread regularity that "we may be led to conclude indeterminate causes as arbitrary individual volition produce next to no effect in modifying social phenomena." [1]

Before long, hopes for a realistic science of society grew dim. Weak statesmen, machine politics, and economic ac-

[1] E. P. Smith, *A Manual of Political Economy* (Philadelphia: Henry Carey Baird & Co., 1853), pp. iii, 18–19; Charles Pomeroy to Rossiter Johnson, October 6, 1888, Johnson MSS, New York Public Library; Morgan to W. H. Seward, February 16, 1861, Seward MSS.

quisition ruled the day. It seemed to the Pundits that the moral fibre had gone out of national life. The businessmen among them felt the pressure of corporative competition and the need for hardheadedness.

None felt it more than Lewis Morgan, who had once assured himself that "agriculture and manufacture are mechanical and deal with the products of the earth, while commerce is intellectual and deals with man." In the upper peninsula of Michigan, commerce turned into a dull brute. Rival companies spent as much time in suits and countersuits as they did in transporting ore. Property in land was the main form of capital and competition between the companies took the form of land-claim wars. These became especially venomous when, in 1855 and 1856, Congress passed a series of acts in reference to the upper peninsula, patterned after the land grant to the Illinois Central Railroad in 1850. Land out of the federal domains was assigned to the state of Michigan to be awarded to persons constructing roads between specified points.

To this feast came entrepreneurs from Cleveland, Detroit, Chicago, Boston, and Rochester, first to go their separate ways and then to clash until the fattest among them drove the others out. During the long series of suits Morgan became the chief attorney for the Rochester interests and used his fees to make growing investments in railroads and mines. In the fall of 1856 the Rochester group organized the Bay de Nocquet and Marquette Railroad Company to build a seventy-mile line connecting both shores of the peninsula. Morgan bought one thousand dollars' worth of its stock. In a second road planned between Marquette and the Wisconsin state line, he invested five hundred dollars. A director and attorney of both, his income grew quickly. By 1863 he bought stock worth ten thousand dollars in a third land-grant road, the Marquette and Ontonagon, and one-fourth the shares in the Lewis Morgan Iron Company of Ishpeming, Michigan, a smelting furnace producing twelve tons of iron daily. By then he was well on the way to a small fortune.

As a railroad lawyer, Morgan labored to gain possession of land warrants awarded by the federal government. Congress provided that on either side of roads alternate sections of land, six sections deep, were to be assigned to companies as each twenty miles was completed, and only if completed within specified periods of time. The Michigan State Rail Road Board certified the construction of each stretch, and the General Land Office in Washington, made the actual award of land certificates. When periods of time allotted for the completion of roads proved insufficient, as during the Panic of '57, or when alternate routes were chosen to facilitate construction, the approval of both offices was necessary. It was frequently delayed for months and even years as one department refused to act before the other. Morgan made frequent trips to Washington and Lansing and his correspondence with both offices grew to staggering proportions.

But most of his legal work derived from the competition for available lands. Rival claimants fought each other in the courts and legislatures of five states. Congressmen, senators, governors, and judges were pressured, bought, sold, and threatened.

In this warfare Morgan soon became a hardened veteran and won the full confidence of his clients. In reference to a "delicate matter to treat upon," one of them wrote Morgan, "I have confidence in your ability and good judgment to conduct a negotiation. You know what is wanted in the matter; and any reasonable arrangement which you can effect will be carried out by myself and associates." His business letters grew to have the forceful and stringent tones of a confident attorney. Between 1857 and 1865 he lobbied five sessions of the Michigan State Legislature, went to Washington nine times, attending one session of Congress continually for four months, and made numerous trips to Chicago, Cleveland, Detroit, and Marquette. In 1865 he finally won an award of a quarter million acres of land for his various clients.[2]

Among other forces undermining the patrician ideals of a Pundit was the rise of applied and professionalized science. In the course of his travels during these active, prosperous years, Morgan met scientists who, like his colleagues in business, concerned themselves simply with practical and immediate problems. They asked few of the large questions once posed by geologists, botanists or biologists. Inventions like the daguerreotype, the magnetic telegraph, the blast furnace, and the reaper seemed to hold no lessons for the theologian and philosopher. A few of the technicians shed the mantle of philosophy with difficulty. Years before, the young Joseph Henry paid so little attention to the practical importance of his electromagnet that he failed to patent it and left the profits from the magnetic telegraph to others. John William Draper turned from his work on the daguerreotype to take up the philosophy of history. But most scientists were pleased with specialization of their crafts and not the least among them were the naturalists. As early as 1847 they led in establishing the American Association for the Advancement of Science and called for a "stronger and more general impulse and a more systematic direction to scientific research in our country." They hoped to procure "for the labors of scientific men in-

[2] H. B. Ely to Morgan, February 7, 1856, Morgan MSS; *Congressional Globe*, 34 Cong., 1 sess., Part 3, 1856, Appendix, pp. 11–12; George R. Taylor, *The Transportation Revolution* (New York: Rinehart, 1951), pp. 94–96; Saul Benison, "Railroads, Land and Iron" (Ph.D. diss., Columbia University, 1953), pp. 122–24, 205–17; Morgan to Peter White, August 1, 1872, Morgan MSS.

creased facilities and wider usefulness." Four years later, the retiring president of the association, Alexander Bache, demanded an end to the view that science was a panacea. "Our real danger lies now from a modified charlatanism which makes merit in one subject excuse for asking authority in others." General science, the plaything of philosophers, must give way to particular disciplines. "The absence of minute subdivision in the pursuit of science, the prevalence of general lecturing on various branches, the cultivation of a literature of science rather than of science itself, has produced many of the evils under which American science has labored, and which are now passing away." Bache had been instrumental in saving the bequest of James Smithson from being used for a library of "higher learning," as proposed by the patrician George Perkins Marsh. In his speech on the subject in the House of Representatives, Marsh compared a laboratory to a charnel house and warned against the cost to wisdom of too much practicality. The appointment of Joseph Henry, then the nation's leading physicist, as the Smithsonian Institution's first director was a victory for the specialists.

In 1856, Morgan attended the tenth annual meeting of the AAAS, which by then included such full-time professionals as Eben Horsford, Jeffries Wyman, James Hall, Louis Agassiz, Asa Gray, Spencer Baird, Benjamin Peirce, and James Dwight Dana. He befriended several of these men, conversed with most, and listened to their precise and systematic papers based on months of research. He was struck by the contrast between these and the amateur writings of the Pundits. Before he left Albany, he joined the association and resolved to take up ethnology again as soon as his business affairs allowed.[3]

[3] American Association for the Advancement of Science (hereafter cited as "AAAS"), *Proceedings,* I (1849), 8; VI (1852), xliv–xlv; XI (1858), xi. "Record of Indian Letters . . . 1859," Morgan MSS; Thomas Coulson,

What time he could spare from legal duties during the next months, he devoted to studying his notes on the Iroquois. Cutting away all extraneous and philosophic observations, he wrote a paper on the essential characteristic of Iroquois society, its distinct laws of consanguinity and descent. He read it before the Club only to perplex its members with technicalities. Chester Dewey remarked that he could see nothing in the subject except the total depravity of the Indian mind.

Requesting a hearing, Morgan was invited to read his paper before the AAAS in August at its eleventh meeting in Montreal.

The League of the Iroquois, he told the assembled scientists, represented a striking form of social organization. It consisted of five nations, each of which contained eight tribes, the Wolf, Bear, Beaver, and Turtle; the Deer, Snipe, Heron, and Hawk.[4] Conversely, each tribe was divided into five parts, one belonging to each of the nations. Originally members of the first four named tribes were forbidden to intermarry, as were those of the last four. Eventually the tribe itself became the exogamous unit. Hawk

---

Joseph Henry, His Life and Work (Princeton: Princeton University Press, 1950), pp. 4, 102–8; David Lowenthal, *George Perkins Marsh, Versatile Vermonter* (New York: Columbia University Press, 1958), pp. 81–93; Donald Fleming, *John William Draper and the Religion of Science* (Philadelphia: University of Pennsylvania Press, 1950), pp. 56–94; A. Hunter Dupree, *Science in the Federal Government* (Cambridge, Mass.: Harvard University Press, 1957), pp. 66–119; Paul Oehser, *Sons of Science* (New York: Henry Schuman, 1949); James D. Teller, *Louis Agassiz, Scientist and Teacher* (Columbus, Ohio: Ohio State University Press, 1947).

[4] AAAS, *Proceedings*, XI (1858), pp. 132–48. Morgan's nomenclature was inaccurate due to his incomplete knowledge of tribal structures. He corrected himself in later years when he substituted the term "tribe" for "nation" and the term "clan" for what he now referred to as the "tribe." The only writer to have noted the classificatory system previously was Joseph Lafitau in his *Moeurs des Sauvages Ameriquains, Comparées aux Moeurs des Premiers Temps* (Paris: Saugrain l'aîné, 1724). Morgan had not read it.

could not marry Hawk but could find a mate among any other Iroquois. Husband and wife therefore always belonged to different tribes.

The crucial phase of this family system was that children were assigned to the mother's tribe, and since all titles, offices, and property were held in it, could not pass out of it, there took place a perpetual disinheritance of the male line. Hence, the son of a Hawk chief did not succeed to his father's office; he did not even inherit his father's tomahawk. But he did obtain his mother's property. The order of inheritance of male offices or tools was through the younger brothers to sisters' sons, since in the Iroquois view these were successively the nearest relations.

A third distinct custom among the Iroquois was their method of describing kin. They merged collateral relatives, described in civil or canon law as uncles, cousins, or nephews, into the lineal line, classifying these as fathers, brothers, or sons. An Iroquois child used the same term when referring to its mother's sisters as it did when referring to its mother. All were equally "mothers," a grandmother and her sisters equally "grandmothers." Conversely, the children of two or more sisters were the "sons" and "daughters" of all, without distinction, and called each other "brothers" and "sisters." The same held true of relatives in the male line.

Morgan explained the use to which this body of facts might be put. In themselves the Iroquois systems of inheritance and kinship classification were little more than curiosities. But he had been told that the same customs existed among the Ojibway Indians of Michigan and among the Creeks and Chickasaws. Missionaries' reports seemed to suggest they might be found among the Micronesian islanders. If it were possible to show their universality among American Indians, it would prove their common descent, and if he could find them in the Orient, he would establish the Indian's Asian origin. Linguists had tried to do both but failed because languages, unlike fundamental institutions, changed too rapidly. He was certain that the subject of his research "bore the imprint of a common mind." [5]

His material could also be used to test the veracity of early chroniclers. Here Morgan initiated his long and bitter dispute with the annalists of the Spanish conquests in the New World. Recently, he told his audience, he had read William Prescott's *History of the Conquest of Mexico*. Based on Spanish sources, the work described Aztec government as a monarchy, complete with nobles, palaces, and serfs. But Prescott himself gave evidence that threw doubt on the propriety of these terms. Montezuma was succeeded to office by his brother Cuitlahua and upon the latter's decease, by his nephew Guatemozin. "Had the researches of this elegant writer brought him in contact with the real institutions of the Aztecs which controlled these questions of descent, he would have discovered, there is every reason to believe, that the people were divided into tribes, with laws of descent precisely similar to those of the Iroquois." Ethnology, as Morgan used it, began to question the veracity of history. He was one step away from using it as a clue to reconstructing the past.

It is uncertain how many of his audience cared to follow Morgan through the complexities of the subject. But obviously he presented a clear and workable hypothesis, and his method was remarkably original. He was, as McIlvaine, who accompanied him to Montreal, remarked, "chartering a new continent of scholarship."

[5] Usually Morgan used the term "primary" instead of "fundamental." "The impress of a common mind" is a phrase that contains the basic assumption of his work until 1865 and from which grew the hypothesis that similar customs reflect common descent. That they may also reflect common or similar necessities and might therefore have developed independently does not appear to have occurred to him before 1865.

Indeed a continent lay between his hypothesis and its proof. In the year that followed he made no progress. As attorney for three railroads and an iron mine, he had little time to devote to research, especially after the start of a business panic in April, 1857. In its wake capital grew scarce, construction of the roads in Upper Michigan halted, and the chances of completion in time for the award of federal land grew slim. Creditors foreclosed property in the Iron Mountain Rail Road and the Federal Land Office refused to approve a change in the route of the Bay de Nocquet and Marquette.

Such business matters took Morgan to Michigan in July, 1858. On the train he met a delegation of Sioux returning from negotiations in Washington and he inquired about their kinship terminology. Though he introduced himself as a member of the Hawk clan of the Senecas, his questions were received with suspicion and embarrassment. But he found some slight evidence of the Iroquois system among them. At Marquette, Morgan spent many hours with the family of William Cameron, a rugged fur merchant married to an Ojibway woman. From Cameron and his sons he received clear testimony that the Ojibway used familial designations similar to the Iroquois, his first direct indication that the Iroquois system was not unique. The experience also taught him the value of frontiersmen and "half-breeds" as informants.[6]

Back in Rochester, he studied Stephen Riggs's *Grammar and Dictionary of the Dakota Language*, recently published by the Smithsonian Institution. Then for the first time since he published the *League*, Morgan visited the Tonawanda Reservation. Among his old friends he inquired

[6] "Notes of a Visit to Marquette, July, 1858," Morgan MSS, entries for July 14 and July 23. It is important that the actual terms used among the various tribes were different, but the principle of classifying certain kin was present.

about the origins of their kinship classifications, but he learned little more than vague legends about a seventeenth-century woman gifted with great foresight, and tales of Ha-yo-wat-ha, a wise man of the Onondagas.[7]

In the weeks that followed he compiled a list of missions and federal agencies in the western territories. He had a seven-page questionnaire and an explanatory note printed, and addressed thirty of these to likely informants throughout the country. Congressman Edwin B. Morgan of Aurora agreed to frank them.[8] During February and March, 1859, missionaries and Indian agents over the continent received Morgan's puzzling letter:

> It has occurred to me, after careful examination of the system of consanguinity and descent of the Iroquois that we may yet be able, by means of it, to solve the question whether our Indians are of Asiatic origin. Language changes its vocabulary and modifies its grammatical structure in the progress of ages, thus eluding the inquiries which philologists have pressed it to answer; but a system of consanguinity, once matured and brought into working operation is in the nature of things, more unchangeable than language; not in the names employed as a vocabulary of relationship, but in the ideas which underlie the system itself. The Indo-European nations have one system identical in its principle features. . . . That of the Iroquois is originally clearly defined, and the reverse of the former. It is at least to be presumed that it has an antiquity coeval. . . .

After explaining the Iroquois terms, the circular requested answers to more than two hundred questions about tribal organization and kinship usage among local Indians, beginning with the designation of one's father and ending with the name of "the daughter of the daughter of a brother to the son of the son of the son of the brother's sister."

[7] Riggs' was one of the first volumes of the *Smithsonian Contributions to Knowledge;* it set a precedent for the institution's publication of ethnological material that was climaxed by Morgan's work in 1871. "Notes of a Visit to Tonawanda, November 6–11, 1858," Morgan MSS.

[8] Morgan to E. B. Morgan, January 8, 1859, January 17, 1859, January 29, 1859, E. B. Morgan MSS, Wells College Library, Aurora. The frank was intended to add authority to the letters.

From Sault Ste Marie, Bishop Baroga answered that others had more time for such questions than he. George Gibbs, a geologist employed on the Northwest Boundary Survey, was similarly inclined. "I have already used all my friends in furnishing material for a work of my own on Indian philology. I am not a believer in the Asiatic origins of the Indians. I think Mister Louis Agassiz right in pronouncing them, like the buffalo and grizzly bear, indigenous." But carefully worked answers came from a mission among the Sioux on the upper Minnesota River. The brilliant linguist Stephen Return Riggs thought Morgan's inquiry interesting and passed on a complete description of the Dakota tribal and kinship systems. It contained many similarities to the Iroquois. Other encouraging returns came from Friend Simon D. Harvey, superintendent of the Quaker mission among Shawnees in Kansas, from Reverend William Hamilton concerning the Omahas in Nebraska, and Reverend Samuel Gorman in reference to the Pueblos of New Mexico.[9] Morgan made arrangements to have further schedules sent deep into the Hudson Bay territory and others to South America. A business trip to Washington gave him a chance to interview a Winnebago delegation. Then he left for his first field trip among the tribes settled in Kansas and Nebraska.[10]

[9] "Letter Asking Degrees of Relationships," draft, 1858; Bishop Baroga to Peter White, March 3, 1859; George Gibbs to Morgan, March 20, 1859; Riggs to Morgan, March 2, 1859, Morgan MSS. The kinship schedules are preserved in the Morgan MSS and are ocassionally still examined by ethnologists. Several letters passed between Morgan and Riggs during the following years and are interesting for the light they throw on Morgan's technique. As he never tired of repeating, his questions were made out so that the schedule was self-correcting, i.e., similar kinship terms were asked for in different ways. Thus Morgan several times insisted that Riggs had committed errors, and a few weeks later would receive corrections from his perplexed informant. See Riggs to Morgan, December 14, 1859, March 8, 1860, April 17, 1860. S. D. Harvey to Morgan, March, 1859, Morgan MSS.
[10] Daniel Wilson to Morgan, March 9, 1859; Morgan to Ephraim Squier, April 6, 1859; George Simpson to Morgan, May 9, 1860, *ibid.*

He arrived in Jefferson City, Missouri, on May 22, 1859, after a five-day journey by railroad. The rails went no further. A steamer took him up the Missouri through un- settled country to Kansas City, where Indians from all over the territory came to trade. Even Pueblos from New Mexico were there. He made arrangements to "ask a good many questions," but next day he started up the Kansas for Topeka.[11] Stationing himself on top of the pilot house, he watched the prairies unfold on either side of the river. All that had been said about them, he noted, failed to express their beauty. Stretching out to the horizon was a "rich carpet of green, green grass looking like a field of wheat in its green state . . . a wonderful spectacle . . . a landscape such as I have never before looked upon." In the distance he watched emigrants, hardy and "nut-brown," making their way to Pikes Peak and the lands beyond. The country was the garden of the world, he thought, and would soon become its granary. Americans could raise cattle enough to feed the whole human race, and the question would soon be what to do with the super-abundance.

Near Topeka, at the Pottawatomie Baptist Mission, he received instructions on how to reach various agencies and the names of persons that might prove helpful. During the next three weeks he traveled over the country between Topeka and Omaha City, walking along Indian trails and "prairie roads" from one reservation to the next, some- times getting rides from emigrants in their covered wagons. Occasionally he hired a guide, as much to carry his twenty- five-pound carpetbag as to show the way. If his compan- ion was Indian, pleasant rests in whatever shade available were spent filling out a kinship chart.

[11] "Journal of a Visit to Kansas and Nebraska, May and June, 1859," Morgan MSS; Leslie A. White, "Lewis H. Morgan's Western Field Trips," *American Anthropologist*, LIII (1951), 11–17.

In the territory north of the Kansas and just west of the Missouri there were seventeen different missions and reservations to which eastern tribes had been removed. With few exceptions the Indians were badly demoralized. Not knowing how to live in the treeless, arid region, they purchased necessities with annuities received from the federal government and then settled into idleness. Agents hoped to make them farmers but each year reported failure to the commissioner.[12]

Most of the tribesmen lived with tragic memories of their lost lands. "It is painful to hear them express these longings for their ancient homes," Morgan wrote in his journal. "They miss the deer and the squirrel and the pigeons of Michigan. . . . I hope before the tide rolls on them they will have become sufficiently advanced in farming to protect and defend themselves." Alcoholism was widespread. A Kaw chief consumed a bottle of whiskey while Morgan questioned him, and when Morgan urged temperance, the Indian replied "that he should drink as long as he lived." Morgan saw Pawnees near Omaha City sell their women for a few pennies and steal whatever they could lay their hands on.

But his trip was a success. On June 22 he embarked for home with eleven schedules in eleven different languages in his pocket. The existence of the Iroquois kinship system was, he thought, implied in eight or ten of them, including those of the Kaws, Shawnees, Delawares, and Wyandottes. His journal contained notes on religious rites, tribal festivals, burial customs, and descriptions of prairie animals and plants. "I return quite satisfied with the general results of my inquiries, only regretting that I could stay so short a

[12] *Report of the Commissioner of Indian Affairs . . . for the Year 1859* (Washington: Government Printing Office, 1860), pp. 15–18, 112–47; Alban W. Hoopes, *Indian Affairs and Their Administration, 1849–1860* (Philadelphia: University of Pennsylvania Press, 1932), pp. 1–34.

time at each place. . . . I have not as much material as I could wish." He laid plans to return the following year.

In Rochester he found more schedules awaiting him. The unity of the Indian race was becoming obvious. "During this period," Joshua McIlvaine later recalled, "he lived and worked in a state of great mental excitement, and the answers he received sometimes nearly overpowered him." Morgan began to inquire for Far Eastern data, sending a schedule to the United States Legation in Japan and another to the Sanskrit scholar, William Wadden Turner. A third went to the missionary Henry W. Scudder of Arcot, India, who was presently visiting in New York.

A month later Morgan rushed into McIlvaine's study breathless and purple with excitement. Throwing some notes on the minister's desk he gasped, "There! What did I tell you!" Reverend Henry Scudder had returned a chart of the Tamil kinship system and as McIlvaine examined it, he saw that it was identical with the Iroquois.[13]

When he published his results ten years later, Morgan explained the change in the scope of his research that followed this discovery:

[It] opened still wider the range of the proposed investigation. It became necessary to find the limits within which the systems of the Aryan and Semitic families prevailed, in order to ascertain the line of demarcation between their forms and that of the eastern Asiatics. The circumscription of one was necessary to the circumscription of the other. It seemed imperative to include the entire human family within the scope of the research, and to work out this comprehensive plan as fully as might be possible. . . . It was evident that the full significance of identity of systems in India and America would be lost, unless the knowledge was made

[13] Joshua McIlvaine, "The Life and Works of Lewis Morgan: An Address at His Funeral," *RHSP*, II (1923), 47–51; Townsend Harris to Morgan, August 15, 1859; W. W. Turner to Morgan, August 7, 1859; H. W. Scudder to Morgan, August 7, 31, 1859, Morgan MSS. As he saw it, Morgan had in hand the first conclusive evidence ever secured that the American Indian population was of Asian origin.

definite concerning the relations of the Indo-American system of relationship to those of the western nations of Europe and Asia and also to those of the nations of Africa and Polynesia.[14]

The proposed study could not be carried out without the financial aid and the authority of a university or of the federal government. Professor William Wadden Turner, among others, pressed Joseph Henry to give Morgan the support of the Smithsonian Institution and to publish his hypothesis before British scholars claimed it. Morgan appealed for aid to Henry and to Spencer Baird, assistant secretary of the institution, during the meeting of the AAAS in Springfield, Massachusetts, where he read a second paper on his researches. He gave hint of a new hypothesis. "With a thread as delicate as a system of relationships, we may yet reascend the several lines of outflow of generations, and reach and identify that parent nation, from which we are, we believe, all alike descended." [15]

In the fall the Smithsonian's directors agreed to print Morgan's charts under the institution's letterhead and to allow him its mailing privileges. From Lewis Cass, secretary of state, Joseph Henry secured a letter to American diplomats in foreign countries calling their attention to the investigation and requesting their co-operation. In January, 1860, the Smithsonian began sending the circular to diplomats on every continent, who in turn usually passed them on to universities or learned societies. Missionaries in the South Seas and on the Asian mainland frequently labored long hours over the inquiry, and a few journeyed into wild regions to seek the answers.[16]

[14] *Systems of Consanguinity and Affinity of the Human Family, Smithsonian Contributions to Knowledge,* XVII (Washington, 1871), 5 (hereafter cited as "*Systems*").

[15] Turner to Morgan, August 7, 1859; "Systems of Consanguinity of the Red Race, Read in Springfield, August, 1859," Morgan MSS.

[16] The letter and circular are in *Smithsonian Miscellaneous Collections,* II, No. 138 (Washington: Government Printing Office, 1862), n.p. Lorrin

In the spring Morgan began to pore over schedules postmarked in Hawaii, Stockholm, Rio de Janeiro, Constantinople, Tokyo, Tunis, Canton, Barcelona, Beirut, Berlin, Calcutta, and Port Natal. These contained the first of two hundred kinship classifications he mastered during the next four years. He tabulated them feverishly and sent Henry lists of further locations to be probed. For a time, he neglected his railroads completely.

In May he made a second trip to Kansas and Nebraska.[17] At the Shawnee mission just west of Kansas City, he met Friend Simon Harvey, who had been among the first to respond to his letters a year earlier. The Quaker had lived among Shawnees for thirty years, following them from Ohio after their removal to Kansas in 1830. He ministered to their needs as best he could and built his mission into the foremost schooling center in the Territory. "No better and no purer man than Friend Harvey lives upon the earth," Morgan thought. By horse and carriage the two roamed for five days over southern Kansas seeking information.

Heading north to Omaha, Morgan completed charts left unfinished the year before. Near Rulo, Nebraska he opened Indian graves in the company of a ferryman, a "large, rough man with red whiskers and yellow hair," who thought Indians, like wolves, beyond "domestication." A trader for the American Fur Company lectured Morgan

Andrews to J. Henry, May 14, 1861, Morgan MSS. See below, chap. vii for the story of Reverend Lorimer Fison of Fiji. Missionaries supplied Morgan with his finest material. They were the first to learn tribal customs and native languages, and some had themselves noticed the peculiarities in kinship systems. Many therefore responded with interest to his letter. It may be conjectured that missionaries were not only the first but also the last to come into contact with many tribal customs before civilization and commerce undermined them. Morgan noted the rapidity with which the kinship classifications of the Iroquois disappeared on the reservations, as did those of the Kansas tribes.

[17] "Journal of a Visit to Kansas and Nebraska, May and June, 1860," Morgan MSS.

on Indian women, and others told him of the abuse and corruption on reservations. Federal agents speculated in annuities, drew up false census reports and pocketed payments intended for tribesmen. The American Fur Company stored government supplies in its warehouses and released them to the Indians only when they brought furs in exchange. Graft, degeneracy, and hate ruled the area, as Morgan described it in his journals.

But away from the reserves, he delighted in the frontier. He traded tall tales with pioneers resting on their way across the plains and copied down stories he heard from them and from hunters, shopkeepers, and hotel managers. Rulo, after all, was Aurora moved a thousand miles west in less than a lifetime.

I omitted to mention that the night before last a ball was given at Rulo. It was got up on short notice. A young man was sent to notify the girls, another to sweep out an empty store and arrange the seats and another to notify the two village fiddlers. At nine o'clock all was ready and the dancing began first with one, then with two cotillions. To secure fair play the gentlemen were numbered from one to sixteen and as all could not dance at once they were called by numbers and made to take their turn.

Among the girls were several halfbreeds, French and Dakota. They were well dressed in English fashion, not omitting hoops; talk our language well and two of them were educated in St. Louis. I joined the dance so far as to dance three times of which twice was with these girls, Miss DeGray and Miss Somebody. They are good dancers and have the manners of ladies. This was my first dance west of the Missouri River.

It was the last ball he attended for many years. The train that brought him west passed others carrying home delegates from the Republican National Convention in Chicago. In towns and villages across the country he had seen banners with Lincoln's name emblazoned on them. On the day he danced the quadrille in Rulo, Southerners met in Richmond to lay plans for a political party of their own.

By the time he returned to Rochester, northern Democrats
had nominated Stephen Douglas.

Anticipating Lincoln's election, Morgan thought it conceivable that he might be appointed the next Commissioner
of Indian Affairs. The conditions in Kansas convinced him
that a trained ethnologist and an honest man was needed
in the Indian office. It was imperative to clean out the
corruption and to establish schools to train the Indians in
agricultural and manufacturing techniques. It was also his
one chance to become a professional scientist, the Bache
of ethnology. Since his last application for a federal appointment, he had learned a few rules of politics.

With the aid of influential friends, Morgan secured the
Republican nomination for state assemblyman from Monroe County's Second District.[18] He waged an uninspired
campaign, proclaiming little more than his support of the
Erie Canal interests and admitting that he should really
not be in politics.

> I can set up no claim to your suffrages, for I have generally
> been a lazy Republican, taking but little part in political contests.
> But I have always felt a lively interest in the success of the principles
> of the Republican Party and hereafter when there is anything to
> be done, I desire to be counted in. (*cheers*)

He won by a small majority and in January took his seat
in the assembly. In the face of the growing secession movement in the South, he joined other assemblymen in pledging
full support to the Union. On January 7 he introduced a
lengthy resolution to that effect, then turned to promoting
his ambitions. Appointed chairman of the Committee on
Claims, he persuaded the chairman of the Committee on

[18] Morgan to Seward, February 16, 1861, Seward MSS. "I am a candidate
for Commissioner of Indian Affairs and it was with a view to promote that
end that I came here [the New York State Assembly] as a member." Morgan to E. B. Morgan, February 19, 1861, E. B. Morgan MSS, Wells College Library, Aurora, N.Y.

Indian Affairs to exchange positions with him and secured the approval of the assembly for the action.[19]

In the meantime the President-elect was flooded with letters recommending Morgan for Commissioner of Indian Affairs. Old friends were persuaded to join the campaign. From Galena, Illinois, Ely Parker, now a federal construction superintendent who was spending many hours with a clerk named Ulysses S. Grant, sent a brief recommendation. Peter Wilson, sachem of the Iroquois Confederacy, forwarded another. The Pundits wrote warm testimonials to Lincoln, as did some of Rochester's politicians. In March, thirty members of the New York State Assembly added their voices to the campaign.

A few days after his inauguration Lincoln appointed William P. Dole of Indiana commissioner. The office had been promised to Dole during the Republican convention in Chicago by Judge David Davis, Lincoln's campaign manager, as part of a bargain that swung the state to the victor. It was a severe blow to Morgan. His interest in assembly affairs declined rapidly. He took frequent leaves of absence and, when present, did little more than correct the wording of bills under discussion.[20]

In July he made a third field trip, this time up the Red River as far north as Pembina and Fort Garry, and during the journey obtained his one hundred and eighty-fifth kinship schedule.[21]

On his return he spent many hours in his study poring over his charts and puzzling over the seeming unreality of current events. The inability to accustom his mind to the

[19] *Rochester Democrat and American,* October 13, 23, 26, 27, 1860; *Journal of the New York State Assembly,* 84 Sess., 1861, pp. 50–51, 273.

[20] Copies of thirty testimonials are in Morgan MSS. Harry J. Carman and Reinhard Luthin, *Lincoln and the Patronage* (New York: Columbia University Press, 1943), pp. 75–76; *Journal* . . . , pp. 122, 135, 154, 188.

[21] "Journal of a Visit to Pembina and Fort Garry on the Red River of the North, July and August 1861," Morgan MSS.

presence of civil war was not unique. In July, 1861, word circulated in Washington, D.C., that General Irving Mc-Dowell was about to advance against a Confederate force stationed at Manassas Junction in Virginia. Hundreds of the city's resident made their way to Centerville on a clear Sunday morning and, stationed on a hill overlooking Bull Run, prepared to watch the spectacle. In the afternoon Virginia's General "Stonewall" Jackson won his *sobriquet;* in the evening dusk the spectators ran in panic from the carnage that suddenly enfolded them.

Several were taken prisoner by the Confederates. Among them was Morgan's close friend and fellow Pundit, Calvin Huson, Jr., district attorney for Monroe County. He had accompanied Congressman Alfred Ely of Rochester on a visit giving moral support to the Thirteenth New York Regiment composed largely of Rochester men. The two watched the troop movements over Bull Run and as Confederates overran their lookout, neither was able to escape. They were sent to a Confederate prison in Richmond, where Huson died of typhoid fever in November.

When informed of Huson's death, Morgan convened the club at his home and read a memorial.[22] Following the eulogy to the young lawyer, he turned to the events of the past year.

That this rebellion is to fall to pieces and the South again become loyal to the Union, I do not believe. The aberration of her people appears to be total and absolute. We have grown asunder in the very elements of the national life. . . .

But while the unity of our race is lost, there are two other unities of infinitely greater importance which yet remain. These are the unity of our institutions and our geographical unity. . . . The rebels against our government have forfeited, by one act of folly

[22] "Memoir to Calvin Huson, Jr., Read before the Club, November 5, 1861," Morgan MSS; Margaret Leech, *Reveille in Washington, 1860–65* (New York: Harper & Bros., 1941), pp. 97–104; Carl Sandburg, *Lincoln: The War Years* (New York: Harcourt, Brace & Co., 1939), I, 302–6.

and of crime, their privileges, their country and their homes, and they should be expelled by the strong arm from every inch of American soil.

The future historian who shall trace the causes of this rebellion will express more surprise at the lateness of the outbreak, than its actual occurrence in the year 1861. Slavery is an alien institution: and it is our chief wonder that it has maintained itself among us with such vigour to the present day.

In the free states our inborn sense of justice condemns, our sense of thrift disowns and our sense of moral purity abhorrs the institution. That it should exist under the shelter of the American Constitution without awakening hostility was largely impossible. . . .

Nations, willingly or unwillingly, live under the absolute control of fundamental ideas and principles, which work out their results with the certainty and uniformity of physical laws. Our institutions are not created by an arbitrary exercise of intelligence, but they are developed by the subtlety of natural logic, from primary ideas which were wrought into the brains of the race in the infancy of its existence. . . . It is impossible to put an alien institution upon any race in the vigour of its life, and maintain it permanently. The ethnic life of the people must be first subdued. . . .

Having read the Confederates out of the Union and out of his mind, Morgan resumed his ethnological research, hoping to recover reason in a world gone perverse. In the following year he closed his law office. Except for work in behalf of the land-grant railroads, he devoted all his time to proving the unity and Asian origin of the Indian race, and perhaps the unity of mankind.

CHAPTER V

EVOLUTION

In St. Joseph, Missouri, in May, 1862, Lewis Morgan boarded the steamer "Spread Eagle" out of St. Louis and started on the grandest of his western field trips. In the company of Henry W. Reed, agent for the Blackfeet, he was heading two thousand miles north and west to Fort Benton at the foot of the Rocky Mountains, a voyage of forty-five days. The "Spread Eagle," pride of the American Fur Company and the largest vessel on the Missouri, ordinarily did not venture into the shallow rapids of the upper river. But heavy spring rains that year swelled the waters to record levels and her captain, Charles Chouteau, Jr., a manager of the company and a grandson of its founder, hoped for an easy voyage. Three boats accompanied the "Spread Eagle." In St. Louis, Independence, and St. Joseph the fleet picked up about 150 passengers, expecting to deposit some of them near Omaha, where the Platte and the Oregon Trail branched west. The holds were loaded with supplies sent by the Commissioner of Indian Affairs to the tribes of the Dakotas. Troops, aboard to protect the vessel in hostile Indian country, mingled with gold miners, missionaries, adventurers and "mountain men." [1]

"On the whole a well behaved and happy group," Morgan noted after a few hours on ship. "There is some gaming but not of a serious character, and some drinking but no drunkeness as yet. The trip promises to be a good and

[1] *Report of the Commissioner of Indian Affairs for the Year 1862* (Washington: Government Printing Office, 1863), pp. 178–97; "Journal of an Expedition to the Rocky Mountains by the Missouri River in May, June, July, 1862," Morgan MSS.

pleasant one." He looked forward to trailing Lewis and Clark's historic route and to collecting data in Arikara, Cheyenne, Mandan, and Crow villages along the river. Through much of the territory the Indians still lived off the hunt, and in the Badlands tribes fought with one another and with federal troops. Each year the governor of Dakota pleaded for reinforcements against the Sioux. "It is impossible to recover the system of consanguinity and affinity of any people, in its details, if it has ceased to be a living form," Morgan wrote later. Where better find it in its living form than among Indians who still resisted civilization? To make the most of his opportunity, Morgan carried a letter from Caleb Smith, secretary of interior, directing all agents to give him their full co-operation.

A few days later, in Omaha, the adventure turned into a personal crisis, the calamity of his life. He was informed by telegraph that his older daughter Mary lay critically ill and was urged to return at once. In his journal Morgan explained his failure to go back: "I could not reach home under six or seven days, from Omaha, travelling night and day," he wrote, as if pleading before some future court of judgment, "and I felt that the crisis was already past and that my darling child was even now no more, or recovering. What to do and what duty required I could not distinctly see and I resolved to continue on the boat to Sioux City and decide." A few months earlier Mary had fallen from the upper bannister of the Morgan home to the ground floor, a distance of almost fourteen feet. Though she appeared unharmed, Morgan now inferred that her illness was produced by some unsuspected brain injury. Torn between familial duty and desire to finish his expedition, his mind gave way to feverish images of Mary and Mrs. Morgan pleading for his return. But the river beckoned him on. "I ought to return to my wife at once," he confessed to his notebook the next day, "and were it merely pecuniary ends I was seeking, I would do so in a moment." Still the lure of the wild tribal lands to the north was too strong. In Sioux City, the last white settlement on the Missouri, he passed by his final opportunity to return. As the town's few shacks disappeared over the horizon, he experienced a terrible tremor of apprehension and once again he expressed it in writing. "I think it my duty to go on, but am not entirely clear that I am right." [2]

During the next five weeks he gave his entire attention to the winding Missouri. The "Spread Eagle" sailed between rows of cottonwood trees and in the shadow of towering bluffs carved by the river. These gave way to jagged buttes and mesas, the "square hills" of the Dakota Badlands, "the most stupendous scenery I have ever seen." Antelope, elk, and prairie dogs ran ahead of the vessel. Near Fort Clark, at the mouth of the Little Missouri, Morgan saw his first buffalo herd, stampeding from the water. Later, hunters killed and dressed down two bulls. At night the "Spread Eagle" tied up while the crew cut lumber for fuel. In the day she was sometimes met by small bands of squalid men and women riding in from the plains to pick up supplies. For thirty-eight cents' worth of sugar and coffee Arikara hunters brought Chouteau buffalo hides scraped, dried, and ready to be sold in St. Louis at four dollars. In Fort Pierre, three thousand Sioux waited for their annuities. A few days after the "Spread Eagle" pushed on, they fought a small war against neighboring bands.

Morgan noted details of Mandan dirt shelters, of a Ree village, of caves, ovens, scaffolds for the dead, and scaffolds for drying hides; he collected rock specimens for Henry Ward, his museum-building friend; he filled his notebooks

---

[2] Entry of May 19, 1862 "Journal." The use of the past tense in the entry suggests it was written to be read in some future time. Morgan to George H. Ely, May 21, 1862, Morgan MSS.

with descriptions of Dakota war dances, Crow mourning customs, sleeping habits among the Blackfeet, and Shawnee traditions of heaven. Everywhere he collected the vocabulary of kinship and paid special attention to economic life. "Property given to a person goes back to the tribe from which it came," he was told about the Blackfeet. "Here then is the tribal organization pure and simple at the base of the Rocky Mountains." Hunters and traders who joined the passengers to gamble found themselves submitting to Morgan's relentless questioning. Robert Meldrum, a former gold miner who had lived twenty-five years among the Crow and spoke their language more fluently than English, proved less informative than his Crow wife. Alexander Culbertson gave Morgan the benefit of his twenty-five years as a fur merchant among the Blackfeet. Gros Ventre horse thieves, on board to escape pursuing Sioux, explained their kinship terms. Father Pierre-Jean De Smet, a Belgian missionary and the most famous and respected one in the territory, described the tribes of the Pacific country. So it went until the "Spread Eagle" reached its destination.

During the last, dangerous part of the ascent, eighty men pulled the boat through narrow shoals and rapids. Within sight of Fort Benton four of the crew drowned as they were swept up by the current. On learning that most of the tribesmen expected at the fort were hunting far in the north, Chouteau deposited his cargo and passengers, turned the "Spread Eagle," and began his descent, drifting as much as twenty miles an hour and two hundred miles a day. "If we escape Indians and sand bars," Morgan noted, "it will be a quick trip down."

In Sioux City he was informed of the death of both his daughters from scarlet fever. A brief entry concluded his journal: "Thus ends my last expedition. I go home to my stricken and mourning wife, a miserable and destroyed man."

He recovered strength and composure during a three-month rest cure in Marquette. Then, returning to Rochester, he drew plans for an elaborate Gothic mausoleum of Connecticut brownstone and spent most of the winter in his library, refining the design of the tomb. When the frost was out of the ground, Morgan hired a crew of construction workers and through the entire spring and summer directed their work at Rochester's Mount Hope Cemetery. When finally the structure was completed, it was the most imposing and expensive of its kind in the city.

Suffering terribly from remorse, he resumed work on his book, which near Fort Berthold he had decided to call "Systems of Consanguinity and Affinity of the Human Family." But he threw it off in despair because it continued to remind him of his misjudgment. At times he quite lost the order of events. "I have ever felt that I lost my children in some sense by following this investigation," he wrote Joseph Henry. Such Faustian guilt plagued him during all his future research and added to the intensity with which he carried on his work. Now he decided to make his book a second monument to his daughters and planned a lengthy dedication that would contain a photograph of the family tomb. When the Smithsonian Institution was ready to publish the volume, Henry recoiled from such a public display of sorrow and refused to include it.[3]

For three years Morgan labored on the manuscript of *Systems of Consanguinity and Affinity*, finally sending it off to the Smithsonian in 1865. Kinship studies are by nature difficult, but Morgan's draft was virtually incomprehen-

[3] "Journal of a Visit to Marquette, August, September, October, 1862," Morgan MSS; Morgan to Joseph Henry, September 25, 1863, Joseph Henry Correspondence, Smithsonian Institution, Washington, D.C. (hereafter cited as "Henry MSS"); Morgan to Henry, February 21, 1867. The correspondence between the two over this matter was voluminous but see especially Morgan to Henry, October 15, 1867, Henry MSS. Henry to Morgan, December 6, 1867, Morgan MSS.

sible. In the manner of a lawyer composing a brief, he argued rather than explained its conclusions. Undefined terms and complex theories were woven into chapters that made no sense to an uninstructed reader. Joseph Henry, ready to appropriate generous funds for ethnological publications, studied a few of its fifteen hundred quarto pages and sent them on to Reverend Joshua McIlvaine, then teaching ethnology and philology at Princeton. "The publication of so large a work will be an expensive affair," he wrote the minister, "and I am anxious that its value should be fully established before it is adopted, and that it should not be put to press until it is thoroughly revised. . . ." In a subsequent letter to McIlvaine he expressed doubt about its value.

But McIlvaine, long familiar with Morgan's research, knew that beneath the tangled organization there lay a vast body of knowledge and striking new contributions to ethnology. Morgan had discovered the existence of two radically different methods of reckoning kinship and had classified most of the population of the globe into one or another category. Where philologists were only able to reduce humanity to a dozen or more still unrelated families, Morgan found a unifying principle for the Indo-European and Semitic nations, and another for all the rest. Having proved that the classificatory or Iroquois method of designating family relationships was not unique but existed among well over half the world's population, Morgan took his place, McIlvaine thought, among the century's great scientists. That was also the view of McIlvaine's colleague, Professor William Henry Green, the nation's foremost Hebraic scholar. But both men urged a thorough revision of the text.[4]

[4] The draft is in Morgan MSS. Henry to McIlvaine, April 26, 1865; Henry to McIlvaine, May 26, 1865; W. H. Green to Henry, March 14, 1866, Henry MSS.

Through most of 1866, Morgan reworked his manuscript and then returned it to the Smithsonian, his patience at the breaking point. Asking Henry to publish quickly, he wrote, "It is absolutely necessary that I should be relieved from it and turn my attention to other matters. For nearly nine years I have given this subject almost my entire time, and it will demand more or less of my time until it is printed. It is also necessary for another reason, that I should be forestalled in some of its conclusions. This has already occurred as to one or two points by McLennan's *Primitive Marriage*." [5]

John Ferguson McLennan was a Scottish lawyer with an interest in the early history of Greece and Rome. In the course of his reading he noticed widespread references either to the practice or to the ritual symbol of marriage by capture, the classic instance being the rape of the Sabines. Herodotus, Xenophon, and Plutarch, among other ancient writers, cited similar incidents. George Sand reported that among the people of Berry, France, a bride must shut herself up at home on the morning of the wedding day and the bridegroom must go through the pretense of storming her house and taking her by force. Jacob Burckhardt noticed the same custom among the Bedouins of the Sinai Peninsula, and others found it in such diverse places as India, South Africa, and Ireland.

McLennan explained the origin of marriage by capture and its symbolic survival in folkways by relating it to the killing of female infants among primitive peoples. Such infanticide led to a shortage of women and the consequent rule of exogamy—compulsory marriage outside the tribe. But since savages were forever at war with one another a male could only take a wife from another tribe by force.

---

[5] Morgan to Henry, February 27, 1867, Henry MSS; McLennan, *Primitive Marriage: An Inquiry into the Origin of the Form of Capture in Marriage Ceremonies* (London: A. & C. Black, 1865). See also Morgan, *Ancient Society* (Chicago: Chas. H. Kerr & Co., 1910), pp. 516–31.

Writing five years after the appearance of *The Origin of Species*, McLennan went on to suggest that marriage by capture had evolved from an earlier custom of polyandry, the possession in common of a wife by several men. It also relieved the shortage of females. A higher stage of polyandry was the possession of the same wife by several brothers. McLennan thought the levirate a symbolic survival of this custom.

Under polyandry, consanguinity could only be known through one's mother. Therefore female kinship characterized all polyandrous, and eventually exogamous, tribes. One of McLennan's proofs was Morgan's circular attesting that among the Iroquois, children did not distinguish between their father and his brothers.

Years later Morgan subjected McLennan's work to a profound critique. He argued that no people were simply exogamous. With the Iroquois, for example, exogamy and endogamy existed side by side. A Hawk could not marry a Hawk but might marry any other Iroquois. While McLennan hypothesized these two rules of marriage as legal principles that were mutually exclusive, Morgan had found them in the field, more than ten years earlier, as two parts of an organic whole.

But in 1865 McLennan had anticipated Morgan on several points not yet in the draft of Morgan's manuscript. A full year before the publication of *Primitive Marriage*, Morgan had a surprising conversation with Reverend Joshua McIlvaine. The minister, an accomplished Sanskrit scholar, was one of the few who really understood Morgan's kinship studies. In 1859 he had presented six lectures on language and ethnology at the Smithsonian Institution and in the following year left the pulpit of Rochester's First Presbyterian Church to teach at Princeton.[6] But the kindly

---

[6] "Joshua Hall McIlvaine," *Appleton's Cyclopedia of American Biography*, VI (New York: D. Appleton & Co., 1888); McIlvaine to Morgan, April 30, 1869, Morgan MSS.

man missed his flock and the warm company of the Pundits, among whom Morgan was his favorite. "I would
rather live in Rochester and near you than anywhere else,"
he wrote Morgan. At least once a year he returned to the
city, and the two spent long hours talking politics, religion,
and science. During one such conversation in 1864, McIlvaine suggested that Morgan's research pointed to some
important questions. The classificatory system of designating kin, which failed to distinguish between the offspring
of several brothers or of sisters, was characteristic, Morgan
had shown, of over half the world. What caused so widespread a phenomenon? asked the clergyman. He proposed
an answer which, on returning to Princeton, he reiterated
in a letter.

MY DEAR MORGAN,
    I have just lighted upon certain references which throw some
light upon the origin of your Tamilian or Indian system of relationships; at least on some parts of it. You remember we were
talking about whether it did not point back to a state of promiscu-
ous intercourse. You will find in Aristotle's politics Book II Chapter 3 where he is refuting Plato's doctrine of a community of wives
this sentence, "Some tribes in upper Africa have their wives in
common," and in a note in Bonn's translation of it the following
references, "For example the Masimanes (Herodotus IV, 172) and
the Ayseuses (Ib. IV, 180). . . .
    I am inclined to think that this state of society might, upon a
full and minute investigation of the remains of antiquity, be found
more extensively to have prevailed than is commonly supposed.[7]

    [7] McIlvaine to Morgan, March 3, 1864. There has been a controversy over
McIlvaine's influence on Morgan, especially in the evolutionary conflict.
See Bernhard J. Stern, *Lewis H. Morgan, Social Evolutionist* (Chicago:
University of Chicago Press, 1931), pp. 22–29, which pictures McIlvaine
as an inhibiting influence holding Morgan back from Darwinism. Cf.
Leslie A. White, "Morgan's Attitude Toward Religion and Science,"
American Anthropologist, XLVI (1944), 218–30, which denies the min-
ister's influence and proclaims Morgan a Darwinist. I believe both authors
misconstrued the relationship between the two, which was extremely
fruitful. Darwinism never came between them, because Morgan's evolutionary scheme was not Darwinist, and therefore unobjectionable to
McIlvaine.

"How stupid not to have thought of that," Thomas Huxley is said to have remarked about natural selection upon first reading *The Origin of Species*. It is likely that McIlvaine's hypothesis had the same effect on Morgan. Years later the minister recalled, modestly but clearly, his own contribution to the development of Morgan's ideas:

During all these years, he had not the least conception of any process of thought in which [the classificatory system] could have originated, or of anything which could have caused it so universally to prevail. He treated it as something which must throw great light upon pre-historic man, but what light he had not discovered. Before the work was finished, however, he obtained and adopted a hypothesis which, rigorously applied to its peculiarities, he found would account for, explain, and render them all intelligible. . . . The reason why people called those their fathers who would not be their fathers now, was because they either were their fathers or were undistinguishable from their fathers, by reason of a common cohabitation with their mothers. . . . The reason why they called them their brothers and sisters who would not be such now, was, either because they actually were such, or were undistinguishable from them by reason of the common cohabitation of their parents with each other. And so of all the other relationships of the system.

The adoption of this explanation of the vast body of facts which he had gathered, worked a complete revolution in the mind of our friend. . . .[8]

Philologists had established the principle that linguistic forms remained in use long after they had ceased to be functional. McIlvaine, assuming the same to be true of kinship terms, deduced that Morgan's strange accumulations of data pointed back to other forms of the family than that based on marriage of pairs.

The idea came more easily to the minister than to the

[8] Joshua McIlvaine, "The Life and Works of Lewis Morgan," *RHSP*, II (1923), 52. In a letter to Joseph Henry, Morgan gives full credit to McIlvaine for suggesting the origin of the classificatory system. Morgan to Henry, July 25, 1867, Henry MSS. McIlvaine does not appear to have read or heard of Johann Bachofen's *Das Mutterrecht* (Stuttgart: Krais & Hoffman, 1861), which proposed the existence of sexual promiscuity in the ancient past and sought to prove it by a textual analysis of Greek literature.

anthropologist. When asked by Henry to evaluate Morgan's manuscript, McIlvaine replied that it led to conclusions not anticipated "and which will, I think, afford a more satisfactory explanation of the superior life of the Aryan and Semitic families, and of the inferiority of the Turanean, than any before known." The stern Calvinist always regarded the tribe as an inferior and degraded form of society. Since savages lacked the Judaeo-Christian heritage, it did not surprise him that they also lacked the monogamous family and the moral code that sanctioned it. Ethnology at best, he might have said, was the study of depravity, and no true Christian need fear the results of its inquiries. The only danger lay in mistaking science for the Faith, and McIlvaine took it as his special duty to warn Morgan against all skeptical writers. When these began to speculate on matters of faith he declared them "shallow! shallow! shallow! The words of Christ reveal to my mind a depth of comprehension of the nature of man and of what constitutes his true well-being to which Herbert Spencer, Darwin, Huxley, Tyndall and the rest of them cannot make the least pretensions. In their several scientific specialties I sit at their feet." But he sat there only for a moment. On reading *The Descent of Man* he bade them farewell: "Man has come up from a low state and there is a splendid future before him. But he never came from the beast." [9]

Morgan pondered McIlvaine's hypothesis for three years before he used it, and he might have withheld it longer had McLennan not been establishing his priority in the field. In addition, Joseph Henry still refused to publish the manuscript and sent it to Professor William D. Whitney of Yale for examination. To Morgan he wrote that "the first im-

[9] McIlvaine to Henry, April 26, 1865, Henry MSS; McIlvaine to Morgan, September 6, 1873, July 17, 1879, Morgan MSS.

pression of one who has been engaged in physical research is that, in proportion to the conclusions arrived at, the quantity of your material is very large." It was then, in May, 1867, that Morgan accomplished his most startling intellectual feat. In a hurriedly written paper he constructed a conjectural history of the human family from "primitive horde," exercising complete sexual promiscuity, through fifteen stages of evolution of the laws of incest, to the modern monogamous family. From each class of kinship terms he received in the course of his inquiry, he deduced the family structure that produced it.[10]

Morgan had recently corresponded with Francis Parkman concerning Parkman's articles in the *North American Review*. Now eager to present his theory and to establish his claims, he sent Parkman a brief description of his paper, then apologized for summarizing a subject that could not possibly be understood without illustration. The trial balloon was well received. Parkman, long an admirer of the *League of the Iroquois*, invited Morgan to present his paper before the Academy of Arts and Sciences in Boston. There, almost a year later, Morgan read his "Conjectural Solution of the Origin of the Classificatory System of Relationship." [11]

An august assemblage that included Asa Gray, Louis Agassiz, Henry W. Longfellow, Noah Porter, Jeffries Wyman, Francis Parkman, and Chauncey Wright received his paper with no overt sign of approval. Agassiz sat stone-

[10] Henry to W. D. Whitney, April 29, 1867, Henry MSS; Henry to Morgan, May 2, 1867, Morgan MSS; "A Conjectural Solution of the Classificatory Systems of Relationships," June, 1867, Morgan MSS.

[11] Published in *The Proceedings of the American Academy of Arts and Sciences*, VII (1868), pp. 436–77; Morgan to Francis Parkman, June 5, 1867, Parkman MSS, Massachusetts Historical Society (hereafter cited as "Parkman MSS"). In a letter to Henry, Morgan requested permission to publish his paper in order to "prevent anticipation." "It will secure me the results of my work and prepare the public for it." Morgan to Henry, March 23, 1868, Henry MSS.

faced, like a bad omen. At the end, no one appeared to show interest, and Morgan left hurriedly, convinced of failure. "It was a rather dangerous experience to go through," he later wrote to Eben Horsford, who had heard him. "Agassiz does not know, nor could the members present fully appreciate the remarkable character of the system. . . . I was afraid to show more lest they would not bear it." Always sensitive to the opinion of others, and perhaps too conscious of the stature of his audience, he quite misjudged his impact. Within a month the academy requested his paper for publication and shortly after elected him to its membership. *The North American Review*, receiving word of his success, invited him to "use its pages to communicate to the public." Boston opened its doors, quietly but surely, and Morgan appreciated the honor. "You have reached a position in Cambridge and Boston in which life itself becomes inspiring," he wrote to Jeffries Wyman.[12]

Joseph Henry, in the meantime, urged by Yale's Oriental Society and Professor Whitney, accepted the manuscript of *Systems of Consanguinity*, now including a chapter upon the evolution of the family, for publication. "There is a pleasure in laboring for an object of laudable ambition which is greatly enhanced by the assurance that the results of our labors is such as to gain the approbation of those who are best qualified to judge of their importance," the director wrote, somewhat meekly and rather clumsily. "I can see that it makes little difference to an institution like the Smithsonian whether a particular memoir is examined, revised and published in two years or in six," Morgan answered. Disagreements over format, dedication, and expense

[12] Morgan to Eben Horsford, February 12, 1868, Morgan MSS; Morgan to J. Henry, March 23, 1868, Henry MSS; Asa Gray to Morgan, May 2, 1868; Morgan to E. Horsford, May 15, 1868; E. W. Gurney to Morgan, November 4, 1868; copy of Morgan to J. Wyman, February 26, 1868, Morgan MSS.

delayed its appearance for four years more. When finally it saw the light of day, the giant volume was the most expensive ever published by the Smithsonian.[13]

Morgan, like others, regarded his ideas as part of the Darwinian revolution. Among members of the American Academy interest in his work was undoubtedly heightened by the belief that he had something to say about the great questions that divided them. And he did. "Your researches are just as convincing to me as Darwin's on man's humble origins," Wendell Phillips Garrison of the *Nation* wrote Morgan a few years later, after the appearance of *The Descent of Man*. Immediately after he received McIlvaine's letter, Morgan purchased a copy of *The Origin of Species* and before he was through with it, the book was well marked up with penciled notes. Later he gave an accurate description of his inaccurate appreciation of it:

> When Darwin's great work on the origin of species first appeared I resisted his theory and was inclined to adopt Agassiz' view of the permanence of species. For some years I stood in this position. After working up the results from consanguinity I was compelled to change them and to adopt the conclusion that man commenced at the bottom of the scale from which he worked himself up to his present status.[14]

Morgan's "bottom of the scale" was only remotely analogous to Darwin's. Following the appearance of *The Descent of Man*, he recognized the difference and the similarity. "Those who adopt the Darwinian theory of the descent

[13] Henry to Morgan, October 5, 1867, *ibid.;* Morgan to Henry, October 25, 1867, Henry MSS.

[14] "List of Books in Morgan's Library," Morgan MSS; Morgan's copy of *The Origin of Species* is in the Rush Rhees Library, Rochester. W. P. Garrison to Morgan, November 7, 1876; Morgan to Lorimer Fison, September 20, 1872, Morgan MSS. For the reception of Darwinism in the United States see Bert James Loewenberg, "The Reaction of American Scientists to Darwinism," *American Historical Review*, XXXVIII (1933), 687–701; "The Controversy over Evolution in New England, 1859–1873," *New England Quarterly*, VIII (1935), 232–57; "Darwinism Comes to America," *Mississippi Valley Historical Review*, XXVIII (1941), 339–69.

of man from a quadruped, and those who, stopping short of this adopt the theory of evolution, equally recognize the fact that man commenced near the bottom and worked his way up," he told the Pundits. "That the early state of man on *either alternative* was one of extreme rudeness and savagism is yet difficult of appreciation." The theory of evolution, he went on to say, did not really belong to Darwin. Ancient philosophers like Horace and Lucretius recognized the fact that man started in savagery and went through a slow and tortuous ascent.[15]

In Morgan's view man was divinely created, separately but indistinguishably from the beasts. He expressed that thought in a book on the American beaver written during the same years as he pored over consanguinity systems. In Marquette during the summer after his journey to Fort Benton, he spent long hours roaming forests and swamplands in search of beavers, since childhood his favorite animals. Reclining against some stump or log for a day at a time and in perfect silence, he watched the man-shy creatures at their work. Each summer following he returned to his observation posts, drew and photographed dozens of dams, and together with his physician, William Watson Ely, dissected hundreds of beaver carcasses. His field laboratory was the richest beaver district in the world, soon to be destroyed by mining and lumber industries. *The American Beaver and His Works,* published in 1868, was regarded at once as the definitive study of the animal. Reviewers compared it to François Huber's books on bees and with Darwin's botanical monographs. Alexander Agassiz abandoned his own unfinished manuscript on the beaver. "As I wrote father it has taken the wind out of my sails completely and there was no necessity of my doing

[15] Morgan, "Roman Genesis of Human Development . . . ," n.d., n.p., Morgan MSS.

anything further at present." Half a century later the
English animal psychologist, G. J. Romanes, called it the
most trustworthy and exhaustive book on its subject.[16]

Few of its readers paid much attention to the last chapter, in which Morgan briefly explained his unorthodox
theory of animal behavior. The beaver and his works, he
thought, offered the finest example of the mental similarities
between man and the beasts; he preferred to call the latter
"mutes." In the building of dams the beaver used thought,
memory and will, and showed a striking capacity for acquiring knowledge. His constructions were similar to some
of man's most primitive inventions, and there was no reason to assume that a different process of mind lay at their
source. The concept of animal instinct insulted both men
and mutes, for it explained nothing about either. Man assigned animals a different principle of mind to explain the
gulf between his intelligence and theirs, but at the dawn
of time the hiatus was hardly perceivable. "For ages, the
bounds of which are unknown, mankind were immersed in
a barbarism the depth of which can be but feebly conceived.
They were without arts, without agriculture . . . there
are glimpses even . . . of a state of society in which family
relations were unknown." At creation, animals and men
were endowed with the same faculties, though in different
proportions so that one advanced more rapidly. But eth-

[16] *The American Beaver and His Work* (Philadelphia: J. B. Lippincott
& Co., 1868). Reviews were in *Nation*, VI (1868), 176; *Atlantic Monthly*,
XXI (1868), 512; *The North American Review*, CVI (1868), 725–27;
American Naturalist, II (1868), 156–58. There are striking similarities in
the two subjects Morgan studied. The beaver, like the Indian, is unique
to the American continent. Although the animal is sometimes found in
Europe, he does not build dams there. Like the Indian too, the beaver and
his works were decimated by the advance of the frontier. See Richard N.
Manville, "The Fate of Morgan's Beaver," *Scientific Monthly*, LXIX
(1949), 187–91. A. Agassiz to Morgan, December 14, 1868, Morgan MSS;
G. J. Romanes, *Animal Intelligence* (London: Paul Trench & Co., 1912),
p. 367.

nology and biology both suggested that at their origin they may have been indistinguishable.

Morgan stopped short of challenging the immutability of the species. As in his ethnological studies, the problem lay outside his purposes and beyond his realm of competence. In his preface to *The American Beaver* he explained that he was concerned with presenting a picture of the social animal in his natural environment and not with problems of classification. That was the fundamental distinction between his realm and Darwin's. One treated social, the other, natural history. The difference became clear to Morgan just as he discovered evolution.

Though he had noted the existence of polygamy, polyandry, and the levirate among tribes in the Dakotas, and heard of their existence elsewhere, Morgan had taken these as local institutions. He could not come upon the evolutionary hypothesis, because unlike McIlvaine, who taught that men are improved by the words of Christ, he had no evolutionary force in mind. Natural law, common sense philosophy, the kinship between man's mind and the beaver's—all these were the static concepts of an eighteenth-century faith that could enfold material progress but not social evolution. It was necessary to give up a life-long habit of looking to the natural sciences for simple analogies as answers to social questions. The difficulty of this parting was the prime reason for Morgan's long delay in applying McIlvaine's hypothesis. But the parting was necessary because nature alone could not supply the explanation for the ascent from degrees of sexual promiscuity to the monogamous family.

Morgan indicated this problem in his lecture before the American Academy. Speaking of the modern family, he said, "Mankind must have raised themselves to this state of marriage after which this form of marriage and not nature teaches the descriptive system of relationships. It is important that this distinction should be noted." It was, because, as he explained a few moments later, it suggested that the "principal customs and institutions of mankind have originated in, and can only be explained as, great reformatory movements of society." The emphasis was on the word "society."

The problem was to discover the realm from which the reform of society grew, and Morgan spent much of the rest of his career on this question. Had his conversion to evolution been a simple incorporation of natural selection into the study of ethnology, he would have become an interesting figure in the history of Darwin's influence, but not necessarily an anthropologist.

"Man works himself up" was a phrase he used frequently. It expressed his image of the evolutionary process as a linear movement, the idea of natural selection being incompatible with the ideal of the homogeneous society. In Morgan's view the fittest led, they did not destroy the weak, and the Kansas prairies, like the top-heavy barges of the Erie, made it difficult to conceive of nature as hostile or miserly. Throughout the fifties Morgan followed the statistics of agricultural production issued by the Commissioner of Patents and sent him data on Rochester's canal and lake trade, local shipyard production, and water power resources. "This is a land of statistics," he wrote the Wisconsin historian, Lyman C. Draper. "Marvellous displays of the laws of population and the events of centuries in the life of ordinary races are traversed by us in a single generation." Like his friend E. Peshine Smith, Morgan agreed with Henry Carey that population growth increases production and wealth and that Malthusian economics was therefore a huge mistake.[17] In the absence of scarcity, evolution was simply a part of progress, and social evolution, like the construction of a beaver's dam, was a co-operative effort between individuals and their environment.

The one economic process Morgan knew from personal experience was the transformation of communal into private property. There was no starker instance of this anywhere than in the granting of public lands to railroads. In regions where Indian tribes once roamed freely, a civilized government claimed, then distributed, natural resources, and finally sanctioned their private ownership. The quest for property in Upper Michigan had destroyed tribal life, brought on corporative wars, and produced marked changes in Morgan's character. Property was obviously a powerful force in human relations.

In his paper before the American Academy, Morgan made only slight reference to economic subjects, but he indicated the direction of his inquiries. If we could assume that men everywhere once lived in the tribal state and failed to distinguish between their offspring, by virtue of the classificatory kinship system, "it will be sufficient to remark, that, if such were the fact, the rights of property and the succession to estates would have insured its overthrow. These are the only conceivable agencies sufficiently potent to accomplish so great a change." In the inheritance of private property, sons must be distinguished from nephews, and nephews from strangers. It was an impressive, original solution. All it needed was elaboration, and proof.

[17] Paul Kosok, "Lewis Henry Morgan on the Flour Mills and Water Power of Rochester," *RHSP,* XXIII (1946), 109–27; Morgan to L. C. Draper, March 13, 1854, Morgan MSS; Joseph Dorfman, *The Economic Mind in American Civilization, 1606–1865* (New York: Viking Press, 1946), II, 789–826.

CHAPTER VI

PRIVATE FORTUNES AND PUBLIC ENEMIES

Morgan was forty-four years old in 1862, when he returned from the ill-fated voyage to the source of the Missouri. In the years that followed he remained robust and active though drained of some of the optimism that once distinguished him. Neighbors observed a "certain sadness, almost solemnness about his nature when one saw him walking up Fitzhugh Street, probably with a number of books under his arm." If he left Rochester for more than a few days, it was always in the company of a relative. He took no more field trips, which since the first visits with the Iroquois had been the marrow of his learning and his great adventures. Now Morgan's library became a retreat from which he ventured with hesitation and only if the benefits seemed irresistible.[1]

During his western journeys Morgan attracted supporters who urged him to go into politics and clean up the Indian department. The most persistent was Reverend S. M. Irwin, a former missionary among the Iowas in Kansas, on whom Morgan had called. Irwin advised him to pay close attention to the next presidential election and "to be sure to support the right man, or the man who may be elected, and then be sure to have everything ready to take charge of the office of Indian Affairs. We must have a change out here." But Morgan knew the difficulties involved in gaining the position and he wanted no more of the machina-

---

[1] Charles A. Dewey, "Sketch of the Life of Lewis Henry Morgan, with Personal Reminiscences," *RHSP*, II (1923), 43. An occasional journey to the Tonawanda Reservation was more a visit with old friends than for the purpose of research; see Manuscript Journals, VI, *passim*.

tions attending it. If he sought public office again it would be for a foreign mission which afforded a chance of meeting scholars abroad and of filling in the weak portions of his kinship charts. Hereafter his scholarship came first, a program that pleased Francis Parkman. "It is refreshing to find in this country at this time one who has the animus and the courage to devote himself to a search after truth separated from questions of immediate social, political and commercial bearing," Parkman wrote him. Andrew D. White also welcomed Morgan into the learned fraternity. Astounded, as he put it, by Morgan's paper on the evolution of the family, he offered him a visiting professorship at the newly established Cornell University. It was an attractive proposal. Morgan would share a lectern with Louis Agassiz, James Russell Lowell, and Goldwin Smith. But he turned it down. His knowledge was too specialized, he decided, and his temper too volatile, for a classroom.[2]

Morgan financed his studies by profits from business. He once estimated that field trips and other expenses in preparation of *Systems of Consanguinity* cost him $25,000. He contributed $1,000 toward the publication of *The American Beaver*. Of all his books only the *League of the Iroquois* paid for itself and brought $250 in royalties.[3]

Through the war years he acted as counsel for the Michigan railroads. He became the most prominent of Rochester's entrepreneurs in the upper peninsula, in part because many of the city's pioneer capitalists despaired of ever garnering profits in that region, and sold their stock to outsiders. In 1865 the federal government made extensive land grants to Morgan's companies, by then controlled

[2] S. M. Irwin to Morgan, December 8, 1862; F. Parkman to Morgan, June 9, 1867; A. D. White to Morgan, October 22, 1868; Morgan to White, October 29, 1868; "I cannot agree with you that teaching is a mean business," J. McIlvaine to Morgan, April 30, 1869, Morgan MSS.

[3] Morgan to Lorimer Fison, June 30, 1879, *ibid.;* In 1877 he advanced $850 towards the cost of publishing *Ancient Society*.

by stockholders to whom the Rochester attorney was a stranger. They were grateful to him for bringing a long process of litigation to a successful close, but not generous in their fees. Years later, Morgan described the poor treatment he received:

> The principal facts are as follows: In 1865, after acting as the attorney of our company for eight years . . . during which time I attended five sessions of the Michigan legislature and one session of Congress (four straight months) besides going to Washington nine times on land office business; also to Lansing, Cleveland, Chicago and Detroit at other times, etc. etc., upon which I had then received all told $2,625, I sent in a final wind up charge of $15,000 in R. R. stock. I had subscribed for $25,000 of the new M[arquette] and O[ntonagon], and had paid in $10,000. I asked for a concession of the balance for my services during the previous eight years. It was a moderate and just sum for the services rendered, and which had secured great advantages to the companies. This was also the opinion of S. P., George and J. N. Ely. I could have recovered twice that sum from any jury on proving the work done: for it included all the legislation for the roads, including exemptions for ten years from state taxation, which saved fifty thousand to each road; the gaining of the Ontonagon land grant which gave the Co. the Champion mine worth a million dollars and saved the Bay De Noquet from being turned into a switch by the C[hicago] and N[orthwestern] and from being finally forced out of our hands at half its value.
>
> They refused me the stock or to pay the amount. They appreciated the results of my labors, because they felt them in their pockets, but as to the man who did the work, they would rather wrong him, as it seemed to me, than treat him honestly and fairly. They objected to my claim *as excessive*. Think of that, Mr. White. You know the principal facts of your own knowledge.[4]

The directors continued to refuse, and after a time, ignored his demands for just compensation. Morgan retained his stock but declined to attend directors' meetings or to act further as attorney for the roads. The loss of his services proved disastrous. The corporations, soon merged into the single Marquette and Ontonagon Railroad, lost all records

[4] Morgan to Peter White, August 1, 1872, Morgan MSS.

in an office fire. Falling behind in the construction schedule provided for in the land grant, the new company was beset by suits only an attorney familiar with its books could argue.

In 1871, faced with the imminent loss of its lands, the board of the M.&O. persuaded Morgan's oldest business associate, Samuel Ely, to appeal to him for aid. Moved perhaps by this demonstration of his value to the corporation and also by the prospect of losing his own share of profits, Morgan accepted the offer.[5]

A rival concern, organized as the Houghton and Ontonagon Railroad and including such powerful financiers as John Jacob Astor, Moses Taylor, Quincy Shaw, George Silsbee, and Charles Francis Adams, Jr., had petitioned the Michigan State Legislature and the Federal Land Office to transfer to it the Marquette and Ontonagon land grant. It also initiated suits charging the Marquette and Ontonagon with breach of contract. For more than a year Morgan and his former law partner, George Danforth, managed to fight the New York and Boston capitalists to a standstill, though they were unable to win a decisive action. Their financial resources depleted, Morgan's clients finally decided to accept an offer for consolidation and with it, loss of control over the resources of the peninsula. Under the articles of confederation the new board of directors was dominated by eastern interests, now the major beneficiaries of the federal land grant. Morgan estimated his share of the loss at ten thousand dollars.[6]

His other business venture, the Morgan Iron Company of Ishpeming, Michigan, a blast furnace smelting 120 tons of pig iron a week, was his prime source of income. As

---

[5] S. P. Ely to Morgan, June 2, 1871, *ibid.*
[6] Saul Benison, "Railroads, Land and Iron" (Ph.D. diss., Columbia University, 1953), p. 281; Morgan to P. White, August 1, 1872; Morgan to Willis Drummond, December 1, 1871, Morgan MSS.

president of the corporation and owner of one-fourth of its stock, he was charged with its management. At least twice a year he journeyed to Ishpeming for this purpose, but left the daily supervision of the furnace to a trusted lieutenant and expert ironmaster, George Donkersley.

For eight years after the war the furnace operated at full capacity, fed by the company's own timberlands and mines, and producing iron that went for highest prices in Pittsburgh. But flush times were over when Jay Cooke and Company, the nation's leading brokers, closed their doors in September, 1873. The panic radiated out of Wall Street and within a month Pittsburgh's steel mills began to shut down. For two years the Morgan Iron Company shipped to a restricted market, selling pig below the cost of production and issuing bonds to the extent of $137,000 at ten per cent. Early in 1876, Donkersley wrote that he was forced to blow out the furnace "on account of my inability to procure money or anything else on the product." In the following year, to satisfy creditors, the plant was sold at auction. By then Marquette, the peninsula's capital, was becoming a ghost town. Everyone was leaving it. Morgan's niece wrote him that only the "few families who have lived on the New England principles of thrift and economy are not hampered with debt and burdened with care and apprehension." [7]

When the panic finally receded, Morgan's New England thrift left him with one hundred thousand dollars and a strong suspicion of businessmen. Only Samuel Ely, his earliest partner in railroading, managed to raid Morgan's purse. He persuaded Morgan to invest in an abandoned copper mine near Marquette because it showed signs of an unworked silver belt. "You are the only one of my old

[7] G. Donkersley to Morgan, June 12, 1869, November 1, 1875, February 14, 1876; Fanny M. Steele to Morgan, May 20, 1877, *ibid.*; Benison, "Railroads, Land, and Iron," pp. 306–14.

friends that has put a dollar into my new enterprise," Ely wrote gratefully. A year later he returned seven hundred dollars because there was reason to "entertain doubts on the subject of the persistence of the belt in carrying silver as it descends" and then left for Utah in a hurry. In Diamond City he urged Morgan to invest again in silver, but Morgan would have no more of it and accused Ely of "being of that class of men by whom panics are made." Protesting, Ely lectured Morgan on the economics of acquisition, but with little success. "It bothers me a little," he wrote finally, "that I cannot make you apprehend the difference between developing, exploiting, producing and speculating." [8]

Behind the demise of numerous entrepreneurs in western New York who had risked capital on the development of inland regions lay the specter of the East, buoyant, aggressive, and operating with irresistible force out of brokerage houses and banks in Boston and New York City. Since mid-century, Rochester businessmen had suffered from the advent of large eastern corporations that had absorbed their holdings in telegraph lines, local railways, mines, and smelting plants. The city's *bête noire* was the New York Central Railroad, which first threatened and finally depleted the canal's carrying trade. Instead of lowering them, the Central raised shipping rates. Symbol of New York City's rising dominance over the economic life of the state and of the alarming growth of monopoly, Commodore Vanderbilt's system first introduced Rochester to the dominant political problem of a new era, government regulation of business enterprise.

For a time the issue lay dormant as the city contended with the politics of reconstruction. The split between Presi-

[8] Ely to Morgan, November 20, 1875, January 3, 1876, November 24, 1876, January 6, 1880, January 17, 1880, February 3, 1880, February 17, 1880, *ibid.*

dent Johnson and radical Republicans, reflected in the state by the editorial battles between Thurlow Weed's *Albany Journal* and Horace Greeley's *New York Tribune*, produced in Rochester a seemingly irreconcilable conflict between two Republican dailies, the *Express* and the *Democrat*. Rival Repubican machines fought with such vehemence for control of the party in Monroe County that each nominated its own candidates and both lost the county to the Democrats in the spring of 1867. Sobered, Republicans cast about for compromise candidates.[9] A "clean slate" grew even more desirable as charges of Republican corruption in the state and national legislatures gained volume. In the fall, "D. D. S." Brown, editor of the *Democrat* asked Lewis Morgan to run for the state senate. The *Express* supported the nomination, then easily put through at the county convention.

Since his term in the assembly, Morgan had stayed out of public affairs, but a few momentary ventures into the political arena were sufficient to bring him to the attention of politicians. He was known as a Radical, opposed to President Johnson and to a soft reconstruction policy. Learning of the capture of Jefferson Davis, he wrote a letter to the press urging that Davis be hanged as a warning to future generations contemplating treason. But if he despised the rebellion, he sympathized with its southern victims. Late in 1866, hearing of the food shortage in the South, he organized the Rochester Committee for the Relief of Southern Starvation. When, in the same year, he took part in drawing up a reform ticket that sought to heal

[9] David M. Ellis, "Rivalry Between the New York Central and the Erie Canal," *New York History*, XXIX (1948), 268–301; Lee Benson, *Merchants, Farmers and Railroads* (Cambridge, Mass.: Harvard University Press, 1955), pp. 18–22; Homer A. Stebbins, *A Political History of the State of New York, 1865–1869* (New York: Columbia University, 1913), pp. 3–83; 267–302. Blake McKelvey, *Rochester: The Flower City 1855–1890* (Cambridge, Mass.: Harvard University Press, 1949), pp. 152–55.

the breach between the city's Republicans, the machines decided he was an obvious compromise candidate for the next election.[10]

Morgan accepted editor Brown's offer in the hope of acceding to the office his father had held some forty years earlier and, as he confided to Joseph Henry, because if Grant were to be elected in the following year, the senate was a possible step to a foreign mission. But he neither understood nor trusted his partners in politics. In turn they regarded him as a useful instrument—clean, but far too abstracted to be taken seriously. "Mr. Morgan has devoted his whole life to the exploration of Indian antiquities," one of them later wrote to Senator Roscoe Conkling, "and has so far by habit of mind linked himself with the aboriginal race, as to render him utterly unconscious of the ordinary events of the prosaic life of the present. . . . No politician or citizen would ever dream of regarding the diction of Lewis H. Morgan on a political matter of slightest value." [11]

It was not a just estimate. Morgan campaigned hard and fought well. At the Republican county convention he made peace with both Radicals and Johnson men by declaring himself in favor of the President's impeachment, but only in principle. In practice, he declared, impeachment would bring a Democratic reaction that would sweep both Radicals and Johnson men from power. During the campaign he withstood terrible vilification from the opposition. He was charged with being a pawn of the Canal Ring and in the pay of other special interests. His backers could do no more than insist he was sound on the "New York Central question" and that "no man can be found who will dare accuse Mr. Morgan directly of participation in

[10] *Rochester Democrat*, May 16, 1865; *Rochester Express*, January 25, 1867; *Rochester Democrat*, October 3, 1866.
[11] Morgan to J. Henry, December 5, 1867, Henry MSS; Lewis Selye to R. Conkling, June 6, 1868, Selye Papers, Rochester Public Library.

any scheme or fraud, public or private." In an election that spelled disaster for Republicans throughout the state, Morgan won by seventy-six votes in seventeen thousand.[12]

Joshua McIlvaine was among the first to send him advice. "I hope as Senator you will feel it to be your special vocation to make yourself heard against the political corruption which now threatens to engulf our institutions," he wrote. "Depend upon it, no government can long continue which has not vitality enough to throw off the diseases to which it is specially incident." Once again the minister's words turned out to have particular significance, for the disease to which he referred plagued Morgan through his entire term in the senate in what was to be one of the stormiest sessions in the history of the New York legislature.

For several years the legislature had been known as "the plaything of the rings." Daily the press reported corruption involving the "canal clique," the "railroad ring," the New York Arcade lobby and a dozen other interests. Shortly before the election Senator Wolcott J. Humphrey of Wyoming County was indicted for stating that he would not support a bill until he was paid five hundred dollars by interested parties. Humphrey, some said, was not less honest, though more frank, than his colleagues. Describing the session of the legislature in which Morgan took his seat, Charles Francis Adams, Jr., wrote that "no representative bodies were ever more thoroughly venal, more shamelessly corrupt and more hopelessly beyond the reach of public opinion than are certain of these bodies which legislate for Republican America in this latter half of the century." Depravity in Albany reached its height in what Adams called,

---

[12] *Rochester Democrat*, October, November, 1867, *passim.*, but especially October 10, 23; November 2, 4, and 6, 1867; October 29, 1869. *Rochester Daily Union and Advertiser*, October 29, 1869.

and in what has been known since, as the Erie War.[13]

A few weeks after Morgan began his term of office, Commodore Vanderbilt of the New York Central made the first of his attempts to buy the Erie Railroad by outright purchase of its stock on the New York Exchange. Erie stock grew scarce and its price rose steadily. The Commodore, straining his resources, continued to buy in a heroic effort to capture control of the only competing road in the state. Just as the corner appeared completed, an avalanche of new Erie paper fell on the exchange, prices crashed, and Vanderbilt was nearly driven to the wall.

His defeat had been managed by the Erie's incomparable treasurer and financial genius, Daniel Drew. Under the General Railroad Act of 1850 a corporation could borrow money in order to finish, improve, or operate its road and to issue bonds for that purpose convertible into stock of the same company. As Vanderbilt's purchases drove Erie to an apparent limit, Drew issued ten million dollars' worth of bonds that were at once converted into one hundred thousand shares and dumped on the market in two equal portions. Vanderbilt, barely able to cover his losses, succeeded in enriching his competitors, who were selling short, by about seven million dollars.

This particular skirmish in the Erie War had special significance for the state legislature and for Lewis Morgan. In April, 1868, the senate appointed a committee to re-examine the railroad act of 1850 and its use by the Erie Company. Within a few weeks the committee reported a bill favorable to the Erie. Soon passed by both houses, it was later compared to an act legalizing counterfeit money. Morgan voted for its passage.

[13] J. McIlvaine to Morgan, November 27, 1867, Morgan MSS; C. F. Adams, Jr., and Henry Adams, *Chapters of Erie* ("Great Seals Books" [Ithaca: Cornell University Press, 1956]), pp. 44–45.

The press charged the legislature with corruption. It was discovered that Erie's Jay Gould had been in Albany during the hearings and, according to Horace Greeley, distributed three hundred thousand dollars to various parties, and as much as twenty thousand to one senator, who wanted one thousand extra for his son. Among several persons implicated during a special Senate investigation was D. D. S. Brown, Morgan's backer and close associate.[14] Asked whether he had employed Brown to help pass legislation, Jay Gould answered:

No Sir. Mr. Brown came here of his own accord, and said his people were very deeply interested in it, and then he went home, and then I telegraphed to him to come back here; I wanted some representative from that part of the state that would know the feelings and sentiments of the people. . . .

Q. Was he employed for compensation?

A. Yes, Sir; I paid him something on account, and told him I would make it right.

Q. How much did you pay Mr. Brown, do you recollect?

A. I think it was one or two thousand dollars.

. . . .

Q. For what purpose did you telegraph him to come here, and pay him the money? What was he to do for the money when he was to come here, and use what influence?

A. He had, in a legitimate way, forwarded the passage of the bill; there were prejudices here against the fact that some of our directors had gone out of the state; it excited a prejudice; and when I came here I found all these prejudices existing and I wanted representatives from different parts of the state to come here, that lived on the Erie road and could explain that everyone who lives on that line of the road are friends of it, and those that live at competing points of the road are friends of the Erie as against the Central. . . .

. . . .

Q. Was it not your aim to obtain persons here from different parts of the state who had, or were supposed to have, influence with particular senators?

[14] *Journal of the Senate of the State of New York*, 91 Sess., 1868, April 19, 20, 21, 1868; New York State *Senate Documents*, V, No. 52 (1869), 28–29; 41–42; New York State *Senate Documents*, V, No. 58 (1869), 3.

A. Well that might have been a result; but my object in getting people here was to represent the sentiment in their locality.

With the exception of Senator Abner C. Mattoon who had actually visited the offices of both railroads before casting his vote and was regarded by everyone as "bought," Morgan came as close to public disgrace as any official in Albany. If Gould bought Brown's influence over particular senators, it could be assumed that in the first place he had in mind the Senator from Brown's own district. Morgan had voted consistently with the Erie bloc and but for the final vote, opposed an investigation of corruption in the legislature.

But his support was not purchased, and he knew nothing of the Erie's payments to the editor. Before his term of office was over, Morgan broke with Brown. Later he aided a fellow senator in a suit charging Brown with malicious slander.

Jay Gould's testimony was accurate in reference to sentiment along the Erie line. In Rochester, a terminal for both railroads, the fear of a New York Central monopoly was so great that to have voted against the Erie was unthinkable. Morgan ran for office on a ticket supporting curbs on the Central. Suspicion of his integrity would have been warranted had he ignored his constituents and voted otherwise. The mystery in the affair was that Jay Gould bought what he already had. And editor Brown obviously missed his calling. In the marketplace his capacity to sell dearly what could be had for nothing might have brought him a fortune.[15]

[15] Matthew Hale to Morgan, October 22, 1869, Morgan MSS. "The city's hope for competitive rates in the east rested on the maintenance of an independent Erie, and the local press sided with Gould, Fisk and Drew in their legislative battles against Vanderbilt" (McKelvey, *Rochester The Flower City*, p. 110). *Rochester Democrat*, April 7, 1868.

During the senate's second session the following year, Morgan made a sustained effort to justify his position in the Erie War. His opportunity came when the standing committee on railroads, of which he was a member, was charged by the senate to re-examine methods of financing railroads and the propriety of issuing convertible bonds in particular. When Jay Gould appeared as a witness, Morgan plied him with questions that made both of them appear as champions of free competition fighting off the dragon of monopoly:

Q. By Mr. Morgan: I will ask you again—I don't know whether it was put in the testimony—what in your opinion would be the effect upon the road of repealing this tenth subdivision of the 28th section of the general railroad law? [Permitting the issue of convertible bonds.]

A. I think it would take away from us the only means we have of developing the road.

Q. What other effects would it have?

A. I think it would lay the state open to a great monopoly—the greatest the world has ever seen.

Q. In what way?

A. It would place all the railroads in the state under one control.

Q. Would you apprehend any serious danger from that source if that section were repealed?

A. That would be the result.

Q. If this section was repealed, who would have a motive to move in this manner against the Erie Railway?

A. Our great competitors are the New York Central and the Pennsylvania Central. Either of them would. . . .

Q. If this section was repealed, you would regard a movement probable on the part of the Central to get control of the Erie?

A. Yes, it would be just what I would do as a businessman; if I had a great many eggs in one basket, and could control a competitor, I would do it; I have no doubt at all, that would be the result. . . .

Q. If the Central had control of the Erie, how far would it give that road a connection west with their present western connection?

A. They would control clear through to the Pacific shore; they would make the price of flour every day in New York or New England a dollar a barrel less or five dollars more; they could make the price all winter long.[16]

Gould could not have asked for friendlier questioning, or Morgan, for a clearer exoneration of his own voting record. But Morgan, not a novice in railroad matters, was aware that the Erie's methods of stock issue, beyond preventing the outright purchase of the road by Vanderbilt, proved extremely profitable to the witness and his associates. As a lawyer he must also have known that it was illegal. The railroad act allowed a corporation to issue convertible bonds in order to expand its facilities, not to rig stock prices. For all the appearance that he gave of an abstracted scholar, Morgan was an eminently practical man. In the absence of efficient state railroad regulation, the maintenance of competition was the only guarantee of reasonable shipping prices. For the time being, defense of the Erie's methods seemed a necessary if unwholesome solution. But to a bland committee report recommending unspecified reforms, Morgan added his own vision of a future legislative offensive in behalf of popular interests:

> The Erie and the Central Railroad Corporation . . . have become formidable financial powers in the state. It is impossible that they should contend with each other by reduced rates, for any long period of time; the tendency is to combination, since they are compelled by the law of self-interest and self-preservation, to work together and to harmonize their relations. It can no longer be either concealed or denied that these corporations have attained a position of power and influence in the State which menaces the interests of the people; they have, in repeated instances and with shameless audacity, attempted to influence by corrupt appliances, the legisla-

[16] New York State *Senate Documents*, V, No. 58 (1869), 122–23. "The strangest thing of all was, that it never seemed to occur to his audience that the propounder of this sophistry was a trustee and guardian for the stockholders and not a public benefactor; and that the owners of the Erie might possibly prefer not to be deprived of their property, in order to secure the blessings of competition." (Adams and Adams, *Chapters of Erie*, pp. 77–78.)

tion of the State and thus attacked the security of the people at the very point, above all others, where it can be most fatally imperilled. The time is not far distant when the people will be compelled, in self-defence, to deal with these corporations to the utmost limits of legislative power . . . the legislature has the power to reduce their freight and passenger rates, to enact *pro rata* freight tariffs, and to amend and repeal their charters. . . .[17]

That was Morgan's final word on the subject. Besides serving as a member of the railroad committee, he presided over the Committee on Engrossed Bills, which gave him an opportunity to rise frequently on the floor and have some slight influence on the order of legislation. He prized most his position as chairman of the Committee on Indian Affairs. As he had during his term in the assembly, he used it to introduce numerous bills in behalf of the Iroquois. He urged the senate to provide for the conservation of timber on reservations, to increase expenditures for Indian education, and brought to the floor a variety of remonstrances from the tribes.

On Grant's election, Morgan decided to apply for a foreign mission. He would have liked to go to Russia to pursue research in consanguinity there, but realized that he lacked sufficient political stature to win the position. Roscoe Conkling presented to Grant Morgan's request for an appointment to Sweden supported by most of the Republicans in the senate and, as Morgan proudly wrote Jeffries Wyman, by testimonials from eleven universities. "But the channels are devious. It takes a politician to row the boat, which I am not." Turned down, he tried for Peru, then China, and finally Italy. For the fourth time he failed to gain an appointment to public office.[18]

Morgan's tenure in the "plaything of the rings" left many

[17] New York State *Senate Documents*, V, No. 58 (1869), 17.
[18] Morgan to Eben Horsford, November 17, 1868, January 5, 1869; Morgan to J. Wyman, February 16, 1869, Morgan MSS. He tried again, unsuccessfully, in 1872.

doubts in his mind about the health of the Republic. As the Grant era wore on and corruption became a byword in politics, his fears increased. From his point of view the worst scandal was that in the Indian department. One of President Grant's first acts was to appoint his comrade-in-arms, Ely Parker, commissioner of Indian affairs. Two years later, Parker was tried by a committee of the House of Representatives on charges of defrauding the government. William Welsh, a Philadelphia merchant, acted as the committee's chief witness. His testimony showed, the committee concluded, "irregularity, neglect, and incompetency and, in some instances, departure from express provisions of law for the regulation of Indian expenditures." There was no direct evidence against the Commissioner, but he resigned at once. Parker was a good man, Welsh wrote Morgan, "but conviviality and a fashionable wife made him the prey of astute and polished augurs." [19]

In spite of such blows, Morgan clung to a faith in the future. To Emily Weed Barnes he remarked that unscrupulous politicians have no real strength, "They are so easily toppled over." But he declined her suggestion that he run again for office and help clean up the mess. Politics was not his game. It was a noble field, he wrote Andrew D. White, "although encumbered with unsavory hindrances, until a certain point of personal preeminence is reached. Then a man becomes a necessity to his party, instead of popularity his necessity." He was not the sort to court popularity, and, in any case, he had started too late. [20]

In June, 1870, Morgan and his wife and their son Lemuel departed for Europe on a carefully planned tour of Britain and the continent lasting fourteen months. The journey

[19] *House Report* No. 39, 41 Cong., 3 sess., 1870–71; William Welsh to Morgan, March 20, 1873, Morgan MSS.
[20] Emily Barnes to Morgan, April 17, 1873, August 27, 1873; Morgan to A. D. White, August 10, 1876, *ibid.*

followed a common itinerary through the cities of Edinburgh, Cambridge, Oxford, London, Antwerp, Brussels, Cologne, Geneva, and over the Alps to Milan, Venice, Rome, and Florence, returning by way of Munich, Vienna, Prague, Berlin, and Paris. It was Morgan's grand tour, the fulfillment of a life-long dream. Tirelessly he spent each day visiting sights, wearing out guidebooks, guides, his wife, and at last himself. In the evenings he spent long hours recording his impressions and the day's events.[21]

The greater portion of his notes resembled an archeologist's decriptions of a lost continent. He made detailed drawings of monuments and noted the dimensions of classic architecture. Setting down everything from the method of serving breakfast in England to the procedure involved in buying a pair of binoculars in Vienna, he had filled, by the time he returned, six husky volumes with closely written, and for the most part useless, observations.

He liked to visit places that he associated with Europe's past glory. A visit to Stratford-on-Avon was a necessary pilgrimage, as was a trip to Bunhill Field, London's burial ground for dissenters. In Venice he recalled how as a schoolboy in Aurora he dreamed of coming to "this city of the sea, with its hundreds of palaces, canals, and gondolas . . . here I am, and today we have ridden through the entire length of the Grand Canal." In Rome, for most of a month, he scaled over the ruins of the empire, rising

---

[21] "Journal of A European Trip, 1870–1871," 6 vols., Morgan MSS. Morgan's European journal has been published in extracts and edited by Leslie A. White in *RHSP*, XVI (1937), 219–389. Morgan wrote a number of articles while in Europe, all of them overly detailed descriptions of famous monuments and public buildings. "You might have given them a real value by giving the impressions made on a man of the West by new sights and scenes," Robert Carter, editor of *Appleton's Journal*, wrote him (Carter to Morgan, May 18, 1871, Morgan MSS). See L. H. Morgan, "Oxford," *Appleton's Journal*, V (1871), 487–98; "Road over the Alps," *ibid.*, VI (1871), 654–57; "The City of the Sea," *Harper's Monthly*, XLV (1872), 481–501.

early each day and returning late at night, pockets filled with sheafs of drawings. Renaissance painting warmed his heart. "Galatea by de Anglis . . . is glorious in splendid beauty. She is substantially nude, tempting a mortal man to climb up and seize her." Mrs. Morgan, a shy and proper lady, did not approve this pagan streak in her husband. In Florence she grew angry at the sight of Titian's Venus and protested its vulgarity. "I tell her it is marvelously human . . . better than the Venus de Medici . . . whose little face has not muscle enough to give a respectable kiss." But for such minor differences they were ideal, enthusiastic traveling companions.

For the current state of Europe Morgan had only scorn. In all countries he noted extremes of poverty and wealth, established privilege, and widespread ignorance. He was pained by the beauty of the English countryside because the land belonged to a few and not the farmers who tilled it. In Austria he was shocked to see women carrying brick and mortar, shoveling coal, and digging along railroad embankments. The poor of Europe, he concluded, were as oppressed as any class in history. "The aristocracy ride and the people carry them by their industry . . . the poor were defrauded of their just rights before they were born."

He saw few signs of progress. In England, the middle classes, far from destroying aristocracy, imitated its rule and its tastes. The Italian peasants were hopelessly degraded. Germany's commercial advances under Bismarck impressed Morgan, but her new government also seemed bent on increasing the wealth of the few. The marrow of Europe's stagnation was the influence of the Roman church, "the advocate and apologist of unequal rights among men, of the rights of kings to govern, of feudalism to seize, and of priests to ravage and burden society." Morgan could not enter a cathedral without commenting on the fanaticism it represented, nor hear of Pius IX without declaring the *Syllabus of Errors* the manifesto of a prince of darkness. In Munich he called on Johann Döllinger on the very day the theologian was excommunicated for his opposition to papal infallibility. The two spent several hours discussing canon law, and the German's confident dignity soothed Morgan for a time. But in Prague the memory of Jan Huss's martyrdom revived his passions. By then he was anxious to get back "under the Stars and Stripes. Our country is the favored and the blessed land."

The solution to Europe's problems appeared in Paris, where Morgan arrived soon after the defeat of the Commune. For several days he roamed the workers' quarters of the city. The remnants of barricades, the marks of cannon and rifle fire, and revolutionary slogans carved into masonry made a deep impression on him. "The Commune, the principles, objects and acts which made up its history, have been unjustly condemned, because not justly understood," he wrote. In the main, he thought, the Communards were honest men, and the government should have made concessions to so numerous and powerful a group of Frenchmen. Though the revolutionaries had committed their share of crimes, he saw the Commune as a footstep to the future. For the moment, he wrote as he was leaving Paris, divine right was giving way to commercial right and governments were becoming instruments for the preservation and increase of property. "Along with this tendency we notice another, namely, that commercial men, as soon as they get money, become aristocrats, and give their influence, such as it is, on the side of the privileged classes. When their day is over, the turn of the people will come. Among European nations it is evidently very distant." Back in

London, he watched a workingmen's demonstration against a proposed parliamentary pension to Prince Arthur. They carry a mountain on their shoulders, he thought, but they are quite certain to persevere.

CHAPTER VII

ANCIENT SOCIETY

Shortly before he sailed for home, Morgan came on a copy of *Systems of Consanguinity* in a London library. Published during his sojourn of the continent, the book had already made an impression in England. McLennan, Darwin, and Sir John Lubbock were reading it, the last preparing to lecture on it before the Royal Anthropological Institute.

To his journal Morgan confessed, "I would like to meet some of the famous men here, but do not see how I can do it without pushing, which I am not inclined to do." But push he did. A letter to Darwin brought a characteristic, curt reply: "We will lunch at one o'clock and you can return by the 2:40 train." The brief visit proved more sociable than the invitation. Darwin talked mostly about the *American Beaver*, which his guest thought fortunate, "as I should have been stranded in the discussion of his great themes." The naturalist had difficulty following kinship charts but thought Morgan's work on the evolution of the family "would stand till the end of time." It was agreed that two of Darwin's sons, soon leaving for the United States, would stop in Rochester with the Morgans.

With Darwin's aid Morgan located John McLennan in London and dined with him several times. On learning that the Scotchman wanted a teaching position and was even ready to teach in America, Morgan sent a letter to Andrew D. White urging him to bring McLennan to Cornell.

A few days later Morgan attended a garden party at Sir John Lubbock's sixteen-hundred-acre estate near Charing Cross. "It was a gathering of the gentry and country squires," he noted. Ladies in full walking dress and gaily colored silks "amused themselves with chit chat . . . and all seemed to enjoy it." Morgan did not, and spent most of the afternoon watching Sir John and his five brothers playing cricket. Before he left London, he also called on Thomas Huxley, "a man of generous and noble sentiments." At the Athenaeum Club he chatted briefly with Sir Henry Maine.[1]

The friendly reception accorded Morgan by English anthropologists did not imply acceptance of his views. Within two years the rising school of British anthropology, led by Lubbock, McLennan, and Edward Tylor, attacked most of Morgan's ideas as unscientific and initiated a long and bitter dispute.[2]

Morgan made a more permanent and startling impression on a humble missionary at the outer edge of England's realm. On returning to Rochester he found a communication from Reverend Lorimer Fison, a minister of the Australian Wesleyan Church. Fison sent a careful description of the Kamilaroi living north of Sydney. They were divided into four tribes and possessed prohibitions on marriage akin to those of other tribal people. But this division was recent, and apparently supplanting an older one. There remained evidence of four pairs of male and female classes. Within each pair every male was considered the husband of every female. The system seemed only a step away from the "primitive horde," and an astonishing verification of

[1] "Journal of a European Trip," V, 91–92; VI, 78–102. Darwin to Morgan, June 7, 1871, Morgan MSS. "Mr. Morgan's book seems to me one of the most suggestive and original works in the philosophy of human progress that has appeared in many years," Lubbock to Joseph Henry, November 8, 1871, Henry MSS. Herbert Spencer to Morgan, February 16, 1872, Morgan MSS, expressed a similar appreciation.

[2] Sir John Lubbock, "Systems of Consanguinity," *Nature* (London), XII (1875), 86, 124–25, 311; John Ferguson McLennan, *Studies in Ancient History* (London: Macmillan Co., 1876), pp. 249–76.

Morgan's hypothesis. The evidence also suggested that the tribe evolved out of a simple sexual moiety.

"Though it may shock the sensitive," Morgan answered the minister, urging him to publish his findings, "the facts are too important to be slighted. You have come upon the great transition period from the communal to the barbarian family." Within a few months he presented Fison's evidence to the American Academy.[3]

Lorimer Fison was Morgan's first disciple. A former student in classics and theology at Cambridge University, he found academic discipline intolerable and, before finishing his degree, sailed for Australia in search of gold. Penniless after several years of prospecting, he joined the Wesleyan church and in 1864 established a missionary school in Fiji. Five years later he received one of Morgan's circulars. He had already noticed peculiarities in the family nomenclature of the islanders and the inquiry started him on a systematic study of the subject. In 1869 he sent Morgan a description of the Tongan family that showed a complete mastery of the difficult concepts involved. Soon he forwarded valuable information about other villages that lay within the bounds of his mission. "I have not been of much use to the world in my time," he wrote to his brother-in-law, Professor Goldwin Smith, then teaching at Cornell, in reference to Morgan's investigation. "He who shows me how to render any good service, however, small, confers a great favor on me." Years later, after publishing his own book and numerous articles on Australian ethnology, he thanked Morgan for the first impulse "to a study which has done me a vast amount of good and given me,

as it were, a second life running side by side and subordinate to that which I had given myself."

As an anthropologist Fison possessed great skill. Though
his purpose as a missionary was to convert the islanders,
his scientific investigations were free of ethnocentrism.
"It takes a civilized man ten years to get out of his own
mindworld and into that of the savage," he wrote Morgan,
and the difficulty of the process led him to remark that
"Satan ought to have set Job to do ethnological enquiries."
He despised colonial officials and took pleasure in horrify-
ing them by comparing their family crests to totems. He
attacked British policy in Fiji, which transformed tribal
chiefs into landlords renting to tenants. Tory notions were
superimposing class distinctions on tribal communes, he
insisted, and one consequence was the introduction of descent through males, "the bottom of all aristocratic notions. Birth comes in as establishing rank, until we get men
who are not 'born' at all, others who are born but not 'fullborn,' others who are fullborn but not 'wellborn,' others
who are wellborn but not 'highborn' and at last men who
are so highborn as to be 'godborn.'" Such wit proved too
much for the colonial elite, who soon snubbed Fison in
public. But it attracted Alfred Howitt, an explorer and
police magistrate for the district of Gippsland, who kept
a picture of Darwin over his bed and joined Fison in his
research.[4]

The Darwinian policeman and the Wesleyan missionary
were a strange combination. Fison's religion conflicted with

---

[4] L. Fison to Goldwin Smith, September 7, 1870; Fison to Morgan, October 4, 1872, December 16, 1872, April 27, 1879, September 14, 1879, March
26, 1880, July 15, 1880, Morgan MSS. See L. Fison and A. W. Howitt,
*Kamilaroi and Kurnai Group Marriage and Relationship, and Marriage
by Elopement* (Melbourne: George Robertson, 1880). Also Bernhard J.
Stern, "Selections from the Letters of Lorimer Fison and A. W. Howitt to
Lewis H. Morgan," *American Anthropologist*, XXXII (1930), 257-90,
419-53.

evolutionary theory, and for almost a year after he sent the description of the Kamilaroi family, Morgan did not hear from him. Then, in a brave letter, the missionary bared the problems that had disturbed him:

Before I go any farther, I will first make one remark for the easing of my mind and of my conscience. I do not know what theory you form as to the *cause* of the gradual advance from barbaric forms of the family; but I can see that those who believe man to have gradually raised himself by his own inherent energy from the profoundest depths of worse than barbarism to the dignity of his present standing on earth, will probably deduce from these kinship enquiries an arguement in support of their theory, taking it for granted that the gradual improvement which has undoubtedly taken place has been development from within; whereas it seems clear enough to me that it must have been the result of a teaching *from without;* the tendency of the human race, individually and collectively, when left to its own devices, having been ever towards worsening and never towards improvement. So that where sceptical philosophers see only man's power, I see and reverently acknowledge the finger of God. I have said this because I have seen from the beginning of my engaging in these inquiries that it would be necessary for me to say it at some time or another to be honest. . . . Having said it, it will not be necessary to recur to it. We can each form his own theory as to the cause, while diligently seeking after the results of the cause. I have no fear as to the final results of any scientific enquiry and there is no cowardice more unreasonable or more shameful than that of orthodox Christians who shrink from or howl against such investigations.

During the ten years of their correspondence, Morgan avoided Fison's frequent questions on the religious significance of their discoveries, although he answered the letter above by admitting his own admiration of Darwin's evolutionary theories. The missionary continued to suffer doubts, especially when further research forced him to wrestle with Morgan's postulate of an original "undivided commune admitting the intermarriage of brothers and sisters." To Morgan's irritation, he stopped short of accepting this for lack of evidence, and because it would offend his colleagues in the ministry. Nevertheless he continued to supply Morgan with invaluable data that appeared to substantiate the concept of the natural evolution of the human family.[5]

Morgan met his second disciple in 1873, when Dr. Martin B. Anderson, president of the University of Rochester, introduced him to Adolph Bandelier, a shy and excessively polite young businessman from Highland, Illinois. Bandelier was brought to the United States at the age of seven by his father, a Swiss army officer, who settled in Highland in 1848 to invest in a bank, a foundry, and a coal mine. Destined to manage all three of these enterprises, Adolph was sent back to Switzerland to attend the University of Berne and to read law. But Alexander von Humboldt, then teaching at Berne, inspired him to study the history of Spanish America. Returning to Illinois, Bandelier relieved his utter boredom with business matters by reading the Spanish chroniclers. He spent all his money on rare books and pored over them late into the night. When he chanced to meet Morgan, he was thoroughly familiar with the literature of the conquests, and the two delighted each other by exchanging their knowledge. "Introducing myself as an obscure stranger, you received me with a kindness I shall never forget," Bandelier wrote Morgan on returning to Highland, and therewith began a correspondence that comprised, on his part, some 160 letters, most of them several thousand words long.[6]

Morgan soon realized that Bandelier was a genius whose capacity for learning languages and absorbing history ap-

[5] Fison to Morgan, May 27, 1872; Morgan to Fison, September 20, 1872 (quoted above, chap. v). In reference to the "undivided commune," Fison wrote, "People think me mad for even hinting at such a thing," Fison to Morgan, February 18, 1874, also May 13, 1880, April 7, 1881, Morgan MSS.

[6] A. Bandelier to Morgan, December 20, 1873, *ibid.* Bandelier's letters to Morgan have been edited by Leslie A. White, *Pioneers in American Anthropology: The Bandelier-Morgan Letters* (2 vols.; Albuquerque: University of New Mexico Press, 1940).

peared to be without limit. He could read a heavy Spanish, Portuguese, French, or German tome in a few hours and explain its contents as if it were a children's book. His knowledge of the Indians of Mexico grew with incredible rapidity. Still he gave his studies only the last portions of his energy. "I am at the office from 7 A.M. to 5 P.M., and have to attend to the coal mine in the spare hours," he wrote Morgan, "and only what is left of the night hours can I devote to study." He despised his work. At one time he dispersed a gang of striking miners, and he was once run out of town because of the failure of his bank. Constantly he complained of lacking "mental force enough to attend to my beloved studies, my life's life." In 1880 he suffered a breakdown from which he did not recover until Morgan secured him a place on an archeological expedition to New Mexico. That began a thirty-year career of research in the southwest, Mexico, Bolivia, and Peru, teaching at Columbia University, and the publishing of numerous works on the Indians of Spanish America.[7]

Long before then he had accepted his mentor's views of ancient Mexican society. Although Morgan's knowledge of the Indians of Hispanic America was limited, he had maintained a dispute with the historians of the Spanish conquests ever since his first paper before the American Association for the Advancement of Science. Morgan believed that the ancient Aztecs were misrepresented by the conquistadors and their historians. In all essentials, he thought, Aztec society was identical with that of the northern tribes

[7] Bandelier to Morgan, May 24, 1874, April 26, 1877, Morgan MSS; E. F. Goad to E. L. Hewett, July 10, 1937, Bandelier MSS, Palace of Governors, Santa Fe, N.M.; C. F. Lummis, "A Hero in Science," *The Land of Sunshine*, XIII (1900), No. 3, 158–65; Thomas T. Waterman, "Bandelier's Contribution to the Study of Ancient Mexico," *University of California Publications in Archaeology and Ethnology*, XII (1917), 249–83; Bandelier's personal journals from 1880 to 1893 (6 vols.; Bandelier MSS, Library of the University of New Mexico, Albuquerque).

typified by the Iroquois. But because the Spanish decribed them in the light of European political experience, they pictured chiefs as monarchs, sachems as nobles, and the majority as serfs. Herein, Morgan believed, began the fancies of the historical tradition that came to full bloom in William Prescott and Hubert Howe Bancroft. "The Mexican field is the one above all others that needs reworking," he once wrote Francis Parkman, "but the story has been so well told and so completely finished that it is next to impossible to overthrow the cunningly wrought fable."

In the *North American Review*, in 1869, Morgan published his first article on the subject. Dissecting nine chronicles of explorations dealing with the legendary seven cities of Cibola, he attempted to show that these fabulous palaces were only communal tenement houses, pueblos, rather than the homes of wealthy nobles. The piece prompted the *Nation* to comment on the poor state of all past American historical writing. Francis Parkman wrote Morgan, "You touch nothing on which you do not throw light." [8]

After meeting Bandelier, Morgan decided to leave him the task of reconstructing the Mexican field. The younger scholar, steeped in Spanish sources, at first resisted Morgan's theories and mustered large bodies of evidence in behalf of the traditional writers. But in 1875, after reading *Systems of Consanguinity*, Bandelier gave way. "All I can say is that in regard to your appreciation of Mexican society, I am fully and squarely your disciple." In the following year he began the revision of Mexican ethnology in three monographs on the Aztecs that were soon published by the Peabody Museum in Cambridge. [9]

[8] Morgan to F. Parkman, June 5, 1867, Morgan MSS; "Seven Cities of Cibola," *North American Review*, CVIII (1869), 457–98; *Nation*, VIII (1869), 358–59; Parkman to Morgan, November 29, 1869, Morgan MSS.
[9] Bandelier to Morgan, September 27, 1875, *ibid*. See *Reports of the Peabody Museum*, X (1877), 95–166; XI (1878), 385–448; XII (1879), 557–699.

Bandelier's conversion encouraged Morgan to make a bristling attack on the old school. Asked by Henry Adams, editor of the *North American Review*, to submit a criticism of the second volume of Bancroft's *Native Races of the Pacific*, Morgan wrote a forty-page article excoriating the dean of Western historians for an "extravagant, exaggerated, absurd, imaginative and reckless" picture of ancient Mexico. Now Morgan extensively used contemporary ethnology to interpret past history, a technique implied by the belief in social evolution according to historical laws. Bancroft's palaces were reduced to communal tenements akin to the Iroquois' long house, nobles became sachems, and, devastatingly, Montezuma's fabulous banquets turned out to be the simple division of the food supply, socially owned and equally distributed among all members of the tribe. The article caused a stir. Francis Parkman sent Morgan his congratulations and support. "How you have gone for Bancroft," wrote Frederick Ward Putnam, curator of the Peabody Museum. "You have taken his scalp off down to his neck." Henry Adams was both impressed and puzzled. "I was much gratified with your 'Montezuma's Dinner' which gave me a strong desire to ask you many questions," and he did, in this and frequent subsequent letters.[10]

By 1875, Morgan was the acknowledged dean of an American school of anthropology. In that year, in Detroit, at the twenty-fourth meeting of the American Association for the Advancement of Science, he established and presided over a "Permanent Sub-Section of Anthropology." A few weeks later he took his seat as the sixtieth member of the National Academy of Sciences.

[10] "Montezuma's Dinner," *North American Review*, CXXII (1876), 265–308. Bancroft published a rebuttal seven years later, *Early American Chroniclers* (San Francisco: A. L. Bancroft, 1883). F. Parkman to Morgan, April 2, 1877; F. W. Putnam to Morgan, August 5, 1876; Henry Adams to Morgan, April 29, 1876, May 4, 1876, May 21, 1876, June 3, 1876, Morgan MSS.

His home became a clearing house for proposed and past research in ethnology. John Wesley Powell, Jeffries Wyman, Frederick Ward Putnam, Horatio Hale, Albert Bickmore, Otis T. Mason, Henry Gillman, and John S. Clark were among the many who came to Rochester to discuss their work with Morgan. Through them he kept abreast of progress in ethnology across the continent. Powell's expeditions into the Rocky Mountains yielded the most recent data on western tribes. Gillman shared his knowledge of archeology along the Great Lakes. Clark continued with the Iroquois where Morgan had left off. Mason knew the Caribbean. Wyman and Putnam led the field in New England.[11]

But the more significant part of Morgan's education now was European. His awareness of advances in scholarship overseas grew during his grand tour, and he realized the relative poverty of American anthropology. "One or two more generations will give us a race of scholars who will equal and I believe excell those of England, France and Germany," he later wrote Asa Gray. "At present they beat us by numbers, by stricter professional education, and by devoting more years of labor to special subjects." He was the only American equal in stature to McLennan, Lubbock, or Tylor and, as he admitted readily, had much to learn from them.

The Europeans were making enormous strides in the field of prehistory, a subject that gained new significance in the wake of Darwin's *Descent of Man* and its conclusive evidence of man's great antiquity. Scholars of every kind and in all countries aided the advance on the ancient past. Danish and French archeologists posited a succession of stone, bronze, and iron ages. Sir Charles Lyell had already

[11] AAAS, *Proceedings*, XXIV, 1875, 337; Joseph Henry to Morgan, April 22, 1875, Morgan MSS. See Morgan MSS, 1874–1877, for the large correspondence he carried on with these men.

led geologists in determining the duration of each age and proposed a geometric ratio in the acceleration of human progress. Theodor Mommsen and Max Müller used philology to ascertain the earliest appearance of various means of subsistence. Since domestic animals, for example, had similar names in Sanskrit, Greek, and Latin, they were presumably known and domesticated before these peoples separated. But language showed no evidence that agriculture then existed.

Henry Maine, the historian of ancient law, concluded that at the dawn of Greek and Roman civilization individual property rights were secondary to those of the community. Johann Bachofen, a Swiss classicist, discovered in Greek mythology strong evidence of the matrilineate and of sexual promiscuity. Its overthrow by monogamy and patrilineality was forcible, he held, and symbolized in the *Orestes* of Aeschylus.[12]

Through the early seventies Morgan also read the German writers Barthold Niebuhr, Otfried Müller, Karl Eichhorn, and Gottfried Hermann. He studied the histories of George Grote and Edward Freeman. Once more he turned to ancient historians and poets, paying special attention now to Lucretius and Seneca.

His interest was not abstract. Morgan agreed with Auguste Comte, Herbert Spencer, and Edward Tylor that contemporary primitive society was arrested in its development and illustrative of the early stages of all social evolu-

---

[12] Morgan to Asa Gray, September 15, 1875, Morgan MSS; Alfred C. Haddon, *History of Anthropology* (New York and London: G. P. Putnam's, 1910); H. R. Hays, *From Ape to Angel: An Informal History of Social Anthropology* (New York: Alfred A. Knopf, 1958); G. P. Gooch, *History and Historians in the Nineteenth Century* (New York: Peter Smith, 1949); Sir Henry Maine, *Ancient Law* (London: J. Murray, 1861); Johann Bachofen, *Das Mutterrecht* (Stuttgart: Krais & Hoffman, 1861); Sir John Lubbock, *The Origins of Civilization* (London: Longmans Green & Co., 1870); Sir Edward B. Tylor, *Primitive Culture* (2 vols.; London: J. Murray, 1871).

tion. The idea was first stated by Thucydides: "many proofs might be given that the early Greeks had a manner of life similar to barbarians today." Therefore, Morgan wrote to Sir Henry Maine, ethnology and prehistory were intimately related subjects and threw light on one another. Maine had become interested in Morgan's researches after his own studies of ancient law. "No doubt the two lines of inquiry promise more and more to connect themselves together," he answered, "and if I am not yet prepared to say the connection has been established, I am quite ready to be convinced." But the connection could not be established empirically, or easily. In spite of evolutionary doctrines, most Europeans lacked Morgan's abiding faith in historical law and suffered from what Bachofen called cultural subjectivity. German scholars, Bachofen wrote Morgan, "propose to make antiquity intelligible by measuring it according to the popular ideas of the present day. They only see themselves in the creation of the past. To penetrate to the structure of a mind different from our own, is hardy work."

As he grew familiar with the works of European scholars, Morgan became convinced of the possibility of a synthesis of their results with his own. Everywhere in history the same brain and physique faced analogous problems of survival, and though some portions of the human family advanced more slowly than others, all must arrive on similar inventions, laws, and institutions. Joshua McIlvaine took this to be a deeply religious view of history, emphasizing God's design and "decidedly the strongest argument in favor of the permanence of the species." [13] But Morgan was traveling on a path between two worlds. "I think moreover," he wrote Joseph Henry, "that the real epochs of

[13] Maine to Morgan, July 30, 1876; Morgan MSS; Bachofen to Morgan, January 4, 1881; McIlvaine to Morgan, June 18, 1877, Morgan MSS.

progress are connected with the arts of subsistence which
includes the Darwinian idea of the 'struggle for existence.' "
He elaborated this thesis in numerous papers and articles
that he now presented before the AAAS, before local historical societies, and in such journals as the *North American Review, The Nation,* and the reports of the Peabody
Museum in Cambridge.[14]

In 1874, Henry Holt, just starting on his publishing
career, suggested to Morgan the issue of a revised edition
of *Systems of Consanguinity.* But Morgan declined the
offer. Lorimer Fison, Adolph Bandelier and American and
European scholarship were pushing him into new realms.
He met all comments on his book by asserting that he was
far ahead of it, and writing a new one. For two years he
hardly ventured out of his library. Then he offered Holt
"something better . . . a new M.S. on 'Ancient Society'
of which I have just finished the last chapter." After several
revisions of the manuscript, Holt published it in April,
1877, and a simultaneous edition by Macmillan appeared
in London.[15]

Ancient Society was a heroic attempt to bring together
the laws that governed man's advancement "from the bottom of the scale" to the threshold of civilization. Morgan
felt competent to deal with four aspects of human progress,
admitting that there were others equally important which

[14] Morgan to Joseph Henry, May 31, 1873, Henry MSS; AAAS, *Proceed-
ings,* XXIV (1875), 266–73, 274–81, 334; XXV (1876), 340; "Indian Archi-
tecture," read before Buffalo Historical Society, June 21, 1876, Morgan
MSS; "Houses of the Mound Builders," *North American Review,* CXXIII
(1876), 60–85; "The Human Race," *Nation,* XV (1872), 354; "Indian
Reservations," *ibid.,* XXIII (1876), 58–59; "Tribe," "Architecture of
American Aborigines," "Migrations of American Aborigines," *Johnson's
New Universal Cyclopedia* (4 vols.; New York: A. J. Johnson, 1874–1878).

[15] Copy of Morgan to Henry Holt, May 29, 1875, Morgan MSS. Final
and preliminary drafts are in Morgan MSS. A second edition was published by Holt in 1878 and a third in 1907. Charles H. Kerr and Company,
Chicago, published a fourth edition in 1910. References below are to the
Kerr edition.

he was not equipped to describe. He first traced the development of the arts of subsistence and the growth of inventions by which men subdued nature. These determined the progress of society through succeeding stages of savagery, barbarism, and civilization. Progress accelerated geometrically, because every item of knowledge became a factor in the further acquisition of techniques. In the lowest stage of savagery, the longest and most difficult period of history, men, like the animals, lived on roots and berries, advancing only after they learned to eat fish and to use fire. The last stage of savagery was initiated by the invention of the bow and arrow and the art of hunting. It terminated with the domestication of animals, the cultivation of grain, and the manufacture of pottery. These commenced the era of barbarism, which closed with the smelting of iron, "the invention of inventions." Writing and commerce were the gateways to civilization.

Each level of advancement marked an ethnic period during which ideas of government, of the family, and of property assumed distinct characteristics. Government, Morgan asserted, has followed but two plans,

using the word *plan* in its scientific sense. Both were definite and systematic organizations of society. The first and most ancient was a *social organization*, founded upon gentes, phratries and tribes. The second and latest in time was a *political organization*, founded upon territory and upon property. Under the first a gentile society was created, in which the government dealt with persons through their relations to a gens and tribe. These relations were purely personal. Under the second, a political society was instituted, in which the government dealt with persons through their relations to territory, e.g., the township, the county, and the state. These relations were purely territorial.

Henry Maine had put the case similarly in his *Ancient Law*. But Morgan's application was revolutionary. Using the Iroquois as the classic example of "social organization," their gentes, phratries, and tribes were shown to be identical with the gentes, phratries and tribes of Greece, with the curia, tribe, and populus of Rome. Fison's Kamilaroi, Bandelier's Aztecs, the Scottish clan, the Irish *sept*, the *thums* of India, and the twelve tribes of the Jews all illustrated a form of society through which man must pass on the way to civilization.

The greater part of *Ancient Society* described the innate characteristics of gentile organization as reflected in its various appearances during history. A society that lacked the concept of individual property, it knew no class distinctions, privilege, or exploitation. George Grote erred in maintaining that early Greek institutions were monarchical. The assumption required a revolution preceding the establishment of Athenian democracy. "No such revolution occurred, and no radical change of institutions was ever effected, for the reason that they always were, and had been *essentially democratical*." Not until land was inherited individually, and landed estates replaced communal farms, was gentile society subverted and a political, territorial government established. A central authority under the sway of nobles met in Athens and usurped the power of tribal councils. In Attica the process lasted centuries, beginning with the legendary Theseus, gaining under Draco and Solon, and drawing to a climax in the establishment of *demes* and of citizenship by Cleisthenes.

In the third portion of his work, Morgan described the evolution of the family. Here he condensed his conclusions on the classificatory kinship system and illustrated five successive forms of exogamy from the primitive commune to the monogamous family. Because descent during eras of sexual promiscuity could be determined only by reference to the mother, the family must first have been matriarchal, as were the ancient gentes.

In a final, brief section, Morgan traced the growth of the idea of property. The passion for its possession grew slowly and in proportion to the amount of wealth available from inventions. In the era of savagery a few rude items, the spear, the flint knife, the fire drill, and the moccasin could hardly generate the "greed of gain." Lands were held in common and tenement houses owned jointly by their occupants. The property of a deceased remained in the gens, the phratry, or the tribe.

The era of barbarism witnessed an increase in the amount of personal property. The cultivation of grains and the domestication of animals, the invention of pottery and weaving, the rawhide shield, metallic tools, and weapons required new rules of ownership. By the time of Solon the society of Attica was still gentile, but most property, including land, was owned individually. Here, in the upper status of barbarism, the monogamous and patrilineal family made its first appearance because the rules of inheritance demanded it.

When finally land could be farmed without limit, "a feeble impulse aroused in the savage mind became a tremendous passion in the splendid barbarian of the heroic age." Now monogamy, having assured the paternity of children, asserted their exclusive right to inheritance, and laid the foundation of personal influence, family ascendancy, and aristocracy.

The great question remained whether the principles of aristocracy, of inequality in wealth and power, would live or die. Several thousand years had passed and only in the United States had privileged classes been destroyed. Then *Ancient Society* closed with ringing sentences:

Since the advent of civilization, the outgrowth of property has been so immense, its forms so diversified, its uses so expanding and its management so intelligent in the interests of its owners, that it has become, on the part of the people, an unmanageable power. The human mind stands bewildered in the presence of its own creation. The time will come, nevertheless, when human intelligence will rise to the mastery over property, and define the relations of the state to the property it protects, as well as the obligations and limits of the rights of its owners. The interests of society are paramount to individual interests, and the two must be brought into just and harmonious relations. A mere property career is not the final destiny of mankind, if progress is to be the law of the future as it has been of the past. The time which has passed away since civilization began is but a fragment of the past duration of man's existence; and but a fragment of the ages yet to come. The dissolution of society bids fair to become the termination of a career of which property is the end and aim; because such a career contains the elements of self-destruction. Democracy in government, brotherhood in society, equality in rights and privileges, and universal education forshadow the next higher plane of society to which experience, intelligence and knowledge are steadily tending. It will be a revival, in a higher form, of the liberty, equality and fraternity of the ancient gentes.

American notices of *Ancient Society* generally regarded it as a profound and definitive work. The *Atlantic Monthly* thought it one of the most important books ever written by an American. The *Nation* condensed "this labor of love by our most distinguished ethnologist" in a lengthy two-part article. The *Pennsylvania Monthly* gave it eleven pages and concluded that "no person ever brought to the study of Greek and Roman institutions so comprehensive and accurate a knowledge of the society and government of savage and barbarous people." The *New York Times* twice reviewed the work of "the philosophical yet sound and sober Dr. Morgan." [16]

Equally impressive was the acclaim Morgan won among scholars. Henry Adams wrote that *Ancient Society* must

---

[16] *Atlantic Monthly*, XL (1877), 374–75; *Nation*, XXIV (1877), 92–93, 107–8; *The Pennsylvania Monthly*, X (1879), 115–25; *The New York Times*, May 19, 1877, August 12, 1877. Other reviews were *New York Tribune*, May 12, 1877; *The Woman's Journal* (Boston), November 10, 1877; *Christian Register* (Boston), February 15, 1879.

become "the foundation of all future work in American historical science." Herbert Spencer regretted that it was not published soon enough for his own use in the *Principles of Sociology*, and Darwin expressed admiration for the great labor that it must have cost its author. Students at the University of Rochester formed an "Ancient Society Club" that met once a week to discuss Morgan's theories. John Wesley Powell read *Ancient Society* long into the night and planned to take it into the field with him. Ferdinand Hayden declared Morgan the "Lubbock of America." [17]

But English anthropologists were less receptive. In a revised edition of his *Primitive Marriage*, John McLennan had earlier attacked Morgan's use of kinship terms as unscientific. Morgan gave a spirited rebuttal in a lengthy appendix to *Ancient Society* but won no concessions from his critic. McLennan wrote a bitter review of the book which led Johann Bachofen to declare, "Historical inquiries do not admit of being treated as cases in a court of strict justice, by reasoning of a barrister. They are matters of observation. . . ." Sir John Lubbock suggested that "in the school of Tylor and Sir Henry Maine, a writer needs more than industry and good will," and called Morgan to task for knowing next to nothing of Egypt, Chaldea, Assyria, and of the Semitic tribes. The consanguine family Lubbock considered an interesting product of Morgan's imagination. Edward Tylor wanted "to say at once what most anthropologists will say, that the author has built up a structure of theory wider and heavier, than his foundations of fact will bear." Differences in theory were at the source of the controversy between Morgan and the English, but it was warmed by personal animosities. McLennan suspected Morgan of lifting ideas from his *Primitive Mar-*

[17] Henry Adams to Morgan, July 14, 1877; Spencer to Morgan, July 19, 1877; Darwin to Morgan, July 9, 1877; Morgan to Fison, March 4, 1880; Powell to Morgan, May 23, 1877; Hayden to Morgan, May 2, 1877, Morgan MSS.

riage. Lubbock and Tylor both strongly disliked Americans. "But," Asa Gray wrote Morgan, "by sufficient raps on the knuckles, we may at length teach our cousins across the water decent attention to what they write about, and manners." [18]

Only *Frank Leslie's Illustrated Newspaper* commented extensively on Morgan's "historic insight into the relations of property to modern civilization." But for these, wrote its editor, "the capitalist and proprietor may be tempted to suppose that the existing forms of property are invested with a certain divine right which gives them a 'right to be' without regard to the sources from which they spring and the social ends which they serve." This was a pungent and reasonable conclusion to draw from Morgan's studies. He had said as much himself in his censure of the Erie War. But the comment missed what John Wesley Powell regarded as the first lesson of *Ancient Society*, that government by the people reflected the normal condition of mankind. Morgan had shown, Powell thought, that monarchy and feudalism were "pathological conditions of the body politic—diseases which must be destroyed or they will destroy—and hence disappearing by virtue of the survival of the fittest. Hope for the future of society is the best loved daughter of evolution." Morgan agreed. "I like what you have so well said about the 'survival of the fittest,' " he wrote Powell. "It is a tremendous thrust at privileged classes, who have always been a greater burden than society could afford to bear." [19]

[18] John Lubbock, "Ancient Society," *The Saturday Review* (London), January 5, 1878; John McLennan, "Ancient Society," *Athenaeum* (London), December 29, 1877; E. B. Tylor, "Ancient Society," *Academy* (London), XIV (1878), 67–68; J. Bachofen to Morgan, May 14, 1878; Asa Gray to Morgan, June 27, 1878; Lorimer Fison to Morgan, February 5, 1880; Morgan MSS.

[19] *Frank Leslie's Illustrated Newspaper*, July 27, 1878; J. W. Powell, "Sketch of Lewis Henry Morgan," *Popular Science Monthly*, XVIII (1880), 121; copy of Morgan to Powell, November 3, 1880, Morgan MSS.

Morgan seemed unaware that the thrust had been his own or of the shift that had taken place in his social philosophy. Years before, the best hope for a classless, homogeneous society had been the unsettled west where workingmen could become capitalists, and small capitalists escape the clutches of large ones. Now it was necessary to "define the relations of the state to the property it protects, as well as the obligations and the limits of the rights of its owners." A future Eden replaced the egalitarian frontier. And, strikingly, terms such as "the struggle for existence" and "the survival of the fittest," though still not used in the Darwinian sense, crept into Morgan's vocabulary.

For Morgan the western frontier was gone twenty years before the census declared it formally closed. His entrepreneurial career in Michigan ended quietly during the very years he was writing his *magnum opus*. The ideal of free, competitive enterprise had received a great blow in the experiences of the Erie War and in the Panic of '73. His image of a future time contained the passions of the Paris Commune. Still, he revised an image, not his politics. His secular religion of progress had undergone a reformation, but American democracy was still its church and the Republican party the keeper of its faith. In 1876 he heartily supported Rutherford B. Hayes.

The closing of the western "safety valve" was not simply the expression of Morgan's personal experiences. For years he had been witnessing the growing brutality of Indian wars. Repelled in his youth by the idea of herding eastern tribes across the Mississippi, he discovered their complete degradation in the course of the Kansas field trips. In 1862 he had sent a series of proposals for the revision of Indian policy and for the reform of the Indian department to President Lincoln. He suggested the creation of two Indian territories, one for eastern tribes, the other for the Plains Indians. The latter, expert horsemen, were to be taught herding to replace their hunting economy. Both territories were to be eligible for statehood. While finishing *Ancient Society*, he wrote an article for *The Nation* containing the same proposals. He now stressed that the western Indians could not be made farmers overnight when the process took thousands of years for Europeans. In 1877 he urged President Hayes to close off portions of the west, especially the foothills of the Rocky Mountains, and to save these for an Indian cattle kingdom. But the heedless conquest continued and proved too much for Morgan. When the gold rush and the extension of the Northern Pacific Railroad into the Black Hills of Dakota brought on the great Sioux War, Morgan defended his lieges. As Custer's last stand at the Battle of the Little Big Horn sounded a call for war across the west, Morgan protested the "hue and cry against the Indian."

> Who shall blame the Sioux for defending themselves, their wives and their children, when attacked in their own encampment and threatened with destruction? . . . Before the summer is over we may expect to hear of the destruction of the great body of these unreasoning and unreasonable Indians, who refuse to treat for the surrender of their lands upon terms they do not approve, and whose extermination may be regarded by some as a merited punishment. The good name of our country cannot bear many wars of this description.[20]

The Indians, he once wrote, "by gratifying the wishes of a stranger," had made his scholarship possible. He could not deny them what remained of the garden of the west.

[20] "The Hue and Cry against the Indians," *The Nation*, XXIII (1876), 40–41; "Factory Systems for Indian Reservations," *The Nation*, XXIII (1876), 58–59; Paul Kosok, "An Unknown Letter from Lewis H. Morgan to Abraham Lincoln," *University of Rochester Library Bulletin*, VI (1951), 34–40; copy of Morgan to Rutherford B. Hayes, August 6, 1877, Morgan MSS.

CHAPTER VIII

AMERICAN SCHOLAR

Following the publication of *Ancient Society*, Morgan experienced a "state of usedupness—which must be a good Saxon word for the condition." He wrote his book with such intensity that he harmed his nervous system. His shaky handwriting alarmed correspondents. He grew depressed and irritable and complained of finding no useful occupation. Again he tried to secure an appointment as ambassador to Italy and failed in spite of impressive support from the academic community. For a time Morgan became interested in the affairs of his church and decided that its congregation needed "righting-up." No one, including Reverend Herrick Johnson of the Auburn Theological Seminary, whom Morgan invited to deliver a sermon at the First Church, understood what troubled the scholar. Morgan's pastor tried a "very *new* Presbyterian and *new* New Testamentary" creed to facilitate his conversion, but got no further than Joshua McIlvaine had earlier.[1]

In the summer of 1878, at the suggestion of relatives, Morgan took a journey through southern Colorado and New Mexico, accompanied by two nephews. One, William Fellowes Morgan, a student at Columbia University's School of Mines, had a fondness for archeology. For three weeks the explorers climbed over such ruins as the great

[1] Morgan to J. Henry, April 11, 1877, Henry MSS; J. McIlvaine to Morgan, June 18, 1877; Dwight Bartlett to Morgan, July 3, 1877; H. Johnson to Morgan, May 11, 1877, July 9, 1877; Charles E. Robinson to Morgan, n.d. (1878), Morgan MSS. Morgan's poor health and "nervousness" were frequently mentioned in letters to him during 1877–80. "Your nervousness is not the result of old age," Morgan's sister wrote him, urging rest. (Harriet S. Porter, September 13, 1878, Morgan MSS.)

Aztec pueblo on the Animas River. They followed the Rio Grande to Taos, riding ponies and wagons during the day, halting at army posts and missions at night, and eating meals at campfires. They slept on canvas and on Indian blankets. This wild and barely explored region, with its splendid relics of the ancient past, burned new life into the sixty-year-old scholar. A supplement to *Ancient Society* stirred his imagination.

On the return journey the troop stopped in St. Louis, where the AAAS convened for its annual meeting. Morgan read two papers on the Indian architecture of the southwest. William read another. Frederick Putnam, permanent secretary of the association, noticed the exuberance with which Morgan introduced his nephews to colleagues. He invited William to Cambridge and promised Morgan to nurture his interest in archeology.[2]

Back in Rochester, Morgan began a new book, a survey of the domestic architecture of the American Indians. He hoped to show that from the long houses of the Iroquois to the adobe and stone "joint tenements" of New Mexico, Guatemala, and Yucatan, the red man's shelters reflected the existence of primitive communism. The pueblos proved conclusively, he thought, that the primitive family could survive only as part of a larger household whose supplies it shared equally and regardless of its status in the community. For over a year Morgan collected daguerreotypes, drawings, and descriptions of Indian domiciles. Again he overtaxed his energy. He completed the book with difficulty and without bestowing on it, as he put it, "the con-

[2] Caroline Morgan to L. H. Morgan, April 23, 1878; W. F. Morgan to L. H. Morgan, April, 1878, September 2, 1878; D. P. Morgan, March 27, 1880, Morgan MSS; Temple R. Hollcroft, "Diary of William Fellowes Morgan," *Scientific Monthly*, LXXVII (1953), 119–28; L. A. White, "Morgan's Journal of a Trip to Southwest Colorado and New Mexico," *American Antiquity*, VIII (1942), 1–26; F. W. Putnam to Morgan, September 13, 1878, Morgan MSS.

tinuous thought I usually give, and which every man should give to a work." *Houses and House Life of the American Aborigines,* a large and profusely illustrated volume, was issued by the Department of Interior in 1881 as part of the U.S. Geographical and Geological Survey of the Rocky Mountains. In publishing it, John Wesley Powell satisfied one of Morgan's oldest desires, to serve the federal government in the capacity of ethnologist.[3]

His renewed interest in Indian architecture led Morgan to sound a call for excavations in the southwest and in Central America. He enlisted support from Charles Eliot Norton, professor of classics at Harvard and chairman of the recently established Archaeological Institute of America. Norton and his group had considerable funds at their disposal, but it was generally assumed that their interest lay entirely in Greek excavations. Although Norton lived only three minutes' walk from the Peabody Museum, he had, according to Frederick Putnam, never been inside it. But the professor responded favorably to Morgan and invited him to draw up a report on the needs of American archeology. Morgan summarized the subject in thirty pages and proposed an expedition to study Indian architecture between San Juan, New Mexico, and the Isthmus of Darien. After long consideration, and to Morgan's surprise, the institute agreed to hire Adolph Bandelier to begin excavations in New Mexico. Later Bandelier was to join the French Lorillard expedition to Yucatan.[4]

[3] *Houses and House Life of the American Aborigines, Vol. IV of U.S. Geological Survey, Contributions to North American Ethnology* (Washington: Government Printing Office, 1881); E. Horsford to Morgan, August 22, 1879, November 17, 1879; Morgan to F. W. Putnam, April 9, 1879; copy of Morgan to J. W. Powell, June 16, 1880, Morgan MSS.

[4] Morgan to Putnam, Jan. 13, 1880; Putnam to Morgan, January 31, 1880; Morgan to C. E. Norton, October 25, 1879, January 13, 1880, January 22, 1880; C. E. Norton to Morgan, January 8, 1880, January 22, 1880; A. Bandelier to Morgan, March 25, 1880; Morgan to J. W. Powell, January 24, 1880, Morgan MSS; Archaeological Institute of America, *First Annual Report of the Executive Committee, 1879–1880* (Cambridge: John Wilson & Son, 1880), pp. 29–80.

Morgan's influence in Cambridge grew. The primitive commune interested "Professor Longfellow's son [who] told us in a conversation night before last of a district in Thibet where all the brothers possess the wife in common," Eben Horsford reported. Oliver Wendell Holmes, Jr., studied *Ancient Society* with care and asked Morgan to comment on his own "Primitive Notions in Modern Law." Frederick Putnam structured his magnificent Indian collection at the Peabody Museum to illustrate the laws of social evolution.[5]

But Morgan had no more confirmed disciple in Boston than Henry Adams. "I am clear," the historian wrote him, "that our American ethnology is destined to change the fashionable European theories of history to no small extent." With this thought in mind, while still at Harvard, he drew comparisons between Indian and Anglo-Saxon law. Had the Indians compensation for personal injury?, he asked Morgan. Had they any notion of a suit at law? What of the "astonishing similarity" between the communal institutions of the American Indians and of the Indo-European races? He had absolute faith in Morgan's scholarship. "On your controversy with McLennan I say nothing. He is hopelessly wrong. . . ." Later, writing Albert Gallatin's biography, he wanted Morgan to evaluate Gallatin's contributions to ethnology. And when finally Adams turned to his great history of the United States, his emphasis on the growth of technology and the development of culture reflected Morgan's theories.[6]

After reading *Ancient Society*, Adams urged Morgan

[5] Eben Horsford to Morgan, February 14, 1876; O. W. Holmes to Morgan, August 9, 1877; John Campbell to Morgan, April 19, 1880; F. W. Putnam to Morgan, December 18, 1876, September 13, 1878, April 9, 1879, January 31, 1880, Morgan MSS.

[6] Henry Adams to Morgan, April 29, 1876, May 4, 1876, May 21, 1876, June 3, 1876, June 17, 1878, Morgan MSS; Ernest Samuels, *Henry Adams: The Middle Years* (Cambridge, Mass.: Harvard University Press, 1958), pp. 293, 303, 362–63.

to initiate a massive study of the North American Indians, utilizing the resources of the Smithsonian Institution and of the various engineering and surveying projects in the west. But Morgan was tired and in turn spurred John Wesley Powell to take on the project. In 1879 Congress established the United States Geological Survey and included a small appropriation for publications in American ethnology. Powell gave Clarence King charge of the survey and established himself in the new Bureau of American Ethnology. As its director, Powell systematized the classification of western tribes and continued the kinship studies started by Morgan. He bought copies of *Ancient Society* wholesale to be distributed among his staff members. Government ethnologists went into the field with Morgan's book and with his kinship charts.[7]

In 1879, Morgan was elected president of the American Association for the Advancement of Science. His election, he wrote Lorimer Fison, gave recognition to the science of anthropology. It was also the highest tribute American scientists could pay to one of their own number. In the spring of the following year, Boston's Academy of Arts and Sciences gave a dinner in Morgan's honor at the home of Eben Horsford. He received a silver lamp to light his way through the recesses of the Indian's past. Moved by the presence of Henry W. Longfellow, Asa Gray, Benjamin Peirce, and others of the city's sages, Morgan murmured a few words of gratitude. "If I had been a 'society man' instead of a provincial," he later wrote Eben Horsford,

[7] Henry Adams to Morgan, July 14, 1877; copies of Morgan to Powell, February 19, 1877, May 26, 1877, October 24, 1877, August 31, 1877, May 8, 1880; Powell to Morgan, February 25, 1880, April 17, 1880, May 11, 1880, Morgan MSS; Wallace Stegner, *Beyond the Hundredth Meridian* (Boston: Houghton Mifflin & Co., 1954); William C. Darrah, *Powell of the Colorado* (Princeton, N.J.: Princeton University Press, 1951). The influence of Morgan's theories in the Bureau of American Ethnology continued under Powell's successor, William H. Holmes. See Holmes, "Biographical Memoir of Lewis Henry Morgan," *National Academy of Sciences, Biographical Memoirs*, VI (1909), pp. 219–39.

I would have made a fine speech to your, let me say graceful presentation of the lamp. But I should have been compelled to admit that the most advanced of my Red Skin friends were below the lamp and watch condition. That while they needed the lamp badly enough to light their dark chambers, to say nothing of their clay pipes, the vision of a silver lamp of such delicate design and workmanship had not dawned upon their minds. The distance of their highest estate to the height of Professor Horsford's dinner party is not fully expressed by the distance separating the terrestial from the celestial. But the red men are not responsible for that. In Yucatan, 350 years ago they were getting ready slowly for the Cambridge dinner.

He had also journeyed long to reach it. On his return to Rochester he was stricken with recurring spells of nervous exhaustion. His speech opening the Boston convention of the AAAS that summer was brief. He bowed to science and commerce and suggested that for one whose homestead lay beyond the Hudson it was pleasant to return to the Athens of America.

Through 1881 he was confined to his home. Unable to see friends and associates without terrible excitement, he was allowed no visitors. He died on December 17, 1881, a month after his sixty-third birthday. Rochester mourned its scholar with fitting dignity. Reverend Joshua McIlvaine preceded his benediction by a brilliant exposition of the classificatory kinship system.[8]

Morgan remained a singular figure in the intellectual history of the nineteenth century. But if in sum his scholarship bore little resemblance to that of other Americans in his day, its ingredients were so common that he never

---

[8] Morgan to Fison, October 16, 1879; Morgan to E. Horsford, May 8, 1880, Morgan MSS; *Boston Daily Advertiser*, August 26, 1880. During the last four months Morgan appears to have suffered complete nervous collapse. "Mr. Morgan is very, very ill, physically and also mentally," Adolph Bandelier recorded in his diary (entry for October 11, 1881, Journal I, Library of the University of New Mexico, Albuquerque). Also Mary Morgan to E. Horsford, September 5, 1881, October 13, 1881; Mary Morgan to J. Bachofen, February 4, 1882, Morgan MSS.

doubted his thoughts were true reflections of reality. That he was wealthy, at times in dissent, a Whig, had little if any bearing on what he *saw* at the base of the Rocky Mountains or in an Aztec pueblo. He would have cast out the notion that subjective, irrational, or subconscious factors made every man his own historian. The laws of nature and society were discovered in broad daylight, not in the recesses of the soul or the musings of philosophers. He attempted to prove this to others—if it needed proof—in his essays on animal psychology that were meant to destroy the "inner principle of instinct." He preferred not to expend time on the study of religion because, as he put it in *Ancient Society*, "religion deals so largely with the imaginative and emotional nature. . . ."

Only a mind in tune with its world could have such confidence in reason. Morgan's social criticisms never subdued his suspicion of reformers. "Hooray for Garfield!" was one of his last political pronouncements. His conservative political allegiances enfolded his social views because the natural environment and evolutionary philosophy contained their own promises. Through most of his life the settling and developing of the west maintained Morgan's hope for economic equality. When the frontier threatened brutally to exterminate all vestiges of the Indian, and of Morgan's romance, he found a second frontier in time. Within his own political philosophy he inferred the elements that "foreshadow the next higher plane of society to which experience, intelligence and knowledge are steadily tending."

Morgan's faith in a science of society surprised few of his contemporaries. His Puritan ancestors, ruled by the immutable will of God, believed that history unfolded according to plan. Through the pages of *Ancient Society*, which recognized few deviations from its pattern of evolution, man stalked as John Calvin might see him, bound to assent to the laws of the universe. The natural law philosophy of the Scottish school reinforced this outlook, as did a lawyer's education in the nineteenth century. Blackstone, Coke, Kent, and Story taught Morgan that positive laws expressed larger principles. Caring less about the creative function of great men than a nation's codes, lawyers were among the first scientific historians. Morgan, like Henry Maine, John McLennan, John Lubbock, Johann Bachofen, and Henry Adams, initially looked to ethnology as a part of comparative law. Preferring to deal with tribal structure, marriage, and inheritance customs, Morgan avoided narrative history. The vacuum, he thought, was filled by the concept of evolution.

The natural sciences also impelled the development of Morgan's views. When he took up the study of kinship systems, the classificatory sciences were at full bloom under the care of Louis Agassiz, Sir Charles Lyell, Benjamin Silliman, Asa Gray, and James Dwight Dana. Morgan saw no reason why classifying social phenomena should not be equally possible. The huge charts of *Systems of Consanguinity* resembled a botanist's handbook, and his scheme of familial evolution had the precision of a geological survey.

For a time reason rebelled against the concept of social evolution. Morgan had to unlearn Reverend Eliphalet Nott's simple lesson that a social order was the expression of natural laws. Moral science floundered in the seas of the classificatory kinship system. But once Morgan believed he had unraveled the history of property, evolution, in his meaning of the term, became a part of common sense. He identified and confused it with the concept of progress. Horace, Lucretius, and Francis Bacon taught him more than Charles Darwin. As men learned and prospered, they changed; in Morgan's day this seemed elemental. Progress could be watched in time as western New York grew from a country of villages into an industrial region. It could be seen in space while traveling west with civilization from Rochester to the Blackfeet commune at the source of the Missouri. Considering the material progress of Morgan's century, why doubt the ancient Greeks were nearer the "bottom of the scale"?

Few really questioned it. Karl Marx, on reading *Ancient Society*, marveled that an American scholar discovered the material basis of history. But Marx's theory had hardly reached the light of day when Thomas Ewbank, United States commissioner of patents, issued reports containing treatises on the fundamental importance of production to the evolution of human relations. Morgan shared with such diverse American spirits as Henry George, William Graham Sumner, and Brooks Adams the assumption that property stands at the bottom of social order. Archeology also posited the relation between tools and the cultural remnants of the ancient past.

Morgan seems a unique spirit because in the midst of great material progress he never appeared to lose his village conviction that "a mere property career is not the final destiny of mankind." There was a streak of rural socialism in the earliest of his romantic meditations along Cayuga's shores. As a patrician Whig he maintained the view that the acquisitive drive was one of the lower instincts. And the alternative to his own, acquisitive career always was the study of the "liberty, equality and fraternity of the Ancient gentes." The uncovering of primitive communism proved to Morgan, as Edmund Wilson has suggested it did to Karl Marx, that economic man was a transient in history. Morgan seemed unaware how sweeping a social doctrine he pronounced in *Ancient Society*, probably because the essence of his socialism was *sociability*, and gentility the prime characteristic of his utopia. In his own day he found these qualities not among Rochester's workingmen, but among the Pundits, and in the company of scholars. Because he feared rather than rejoiced in the class struggle, he pleaded urgently for the social management of property. His vision included the image of Austrian women shoveling coal and the savagery of class war in the streets of Paris.

Since his day, Morgan's reputation has declined rapidly. With the exception of *League of the Iroquois*, his work was too complex to make inviting reading. Endorsement of his theories by Socialists caused some suspicion of his integrity among non-Socialists; the development of anthropology into a more precise discipline cast new lights on his subject. Ideas that his own climate of opinion accepted as common sense floundered in the context of fresh patterns of thought and changing circumstances.

His descent began with the growth of the imperial urge at the end of the century. Some writers have viewed Morgan's evolutionary scheme as a justification of imperialism because it pronounced his own society superior to that of primitives. For Morgan, the anthropologist Paul Radin wrote, "primitive peoples were only pawns in a much larger game." But this was an inaccurate estimate, as expansionists well knew. The theory of imperialism rested on the assumption that backward nations were incapable of progress without the aid of civilized ones. "God . . . has made us the master organizers of the world," said Senator Albert Beveridge,

to establish system where chaos reigns. He has given us the spirit of progress to overwhelm the forces of reaction throughout the earth. He has made us adept at government that we may administer government among savage and senile people. Were it not for such a force as this, the world would relapse into barbarism overnight.[9]

This view of the matter, summarized by Rudyard Kipling as the white man's burden, had nothing in common with Morgan's theory of social evolution. Progress, Morgan emphasized, was inherent in all cultures, civilized or not, and each must advance along its own course. In his letter to President Hayes he wrote, "We wonder why the Indian cannot civilize, but how could they, any more than our own remote ancestors, jump ethnical periods." Civilization was a process; it could not, in Senator Beveridge's terms, be administered. Morgan's theories were useless as imperialist doctrine. During the 1890's they gave way to notions of racial, and consequently permanent, superiority.

A more vital factor in the decline of social evolution was the rise of pragmatic philosophy. In almost every field of learning, pragmatism effected a turn from all rigid systems and social laws that presumed to reflect reality. It replaced certainty with probability, causality with choice. Focusing its attack on Herbert Spencer's cosmology, it cut down all evolutionary "sticktogetherations." The immutable laws of *Ancient Society* appeared absurd in the light of the new criticism, especially after anthropology felt its impact and became, under the guidance of Franz Boas, a brand new discipline.

Born in Germany and trained in Berlin as a physicist, Boas came to the United States in 1888 and became curator for the Museum of Natural History in New York. He began teaching ethnology at Columbia University in 1896, and during the following forty years his seminars grew to be the focal point of American anthropology. Out of

[9] Paul Radin, *The Method and Theory of Ethnology* (New York: McGraw-Hill Book Co., 1933), p. 253; Quoted in Albert K. Weinberg, *Manifest Destiny* (Baltimore: Johns Hopkins Press, 1935), p. 308.

them came the most respected and productive scholars in the field, including Alfred Kroeber, Robert Lowie, Paul Radin, Edward Sapir, Melville Herskovits, and A. A. Goldenweiser. His students brought Boas' teachings and methods of research to almost every large university in the United States, and it is probable that no other academic subject has been so influenced by a single man.[10]

Boas transformed anthropology from a study of man and society into the investigation of specific men living in particular cultures. Suspecting all theory, he stressed the empirical side of scholarship and taught his students to describe, rather than analyze the patterns of primitive life. He warned against any attempts to evaluate another culture, since such estimates could only be made with reference to subjective and extraneous standards. Ethnocentrism became the prime foible of anthropologists. In Boas' view, a society was a self-sufficient and homogeneous unit whose various institutions, laws, and customs could not be understood except in relation to one another and in context of the need that produced them. The ideal form of research, the field trip, grew to be more than an excursion in quest of specific data. Boas' students lived in a Polynesian or African village for months and even years, until they fully appreciated its manner and purpose of doing things. Their reports became the basic units of anthropological literature.

The new school devoted considerable effort to censuring the works of earlier writers, and at times this appeared to

[10] Richard Hofstadter, *Social Darwinism in American Thought* (Boston: Beacon Press, 1955), p. 129; Robert Lowie, *The History of Ethnological Theory* (New York: Farrar & Rinehart, 1937), pp. 54–67, 128–55; Franz Boas, *Anthropology and Modern Life* (New York: W. W. Norton, 1928), pp. 198–236; Franz Boas, *The Mind of Primitive Man* (New York: Macmillan Co., 1911); Melville Herskovits, *Franz Boas* (New York: Charles Scribner's Sons, 1953); Murray Wax, "The Limitations of Boas' Anthropology," *American Anthropologist*, LVIII (1956), 63–75; David Bidney, "The Concept of Value in Modern Anthropology," *Anthropology Today*, ed. A. Kroeber (Chicago: University of Chicago Press, 1953), pp. 682–99.

be its sole function. It refuted all generalizations about the superiority of civilized over primitive life whether cast in racist or sociological language. Morgan appeared to belong in a category with De Gobineau and Houston Stewart Chamberlain, and *Ancient Society* was marked as the essence of ethnocentrism. Iroquois, Aztec, or Australian society was not anterior to civilization because it was not a lower but an alternative form of culture. For the same reason the theory of progress was nothing more than a metaphysical abstraction in the minds of armchair philosophers. Morgan's ethnic stages were ranked as one of its more curious products.

The logic of this approach led to the denial of evolution as a force in the advancement of primitive societies. Insofar as they changed at all, they did so by acquiring knowledge and techniques from other cultures, adapting the useful and discarding the unnecessary. Boas replaced Morgan's social evolution with cultural diffusion.[11] Strangely enough, Rudyard Kipling would not have disagreed.

Although few of Morgan's conclusions escaped the criticism of twentieth-century American anthropology, regard was given to his methods. His initiation of kinship studies

[11] An extensive controversy over this question is now abating. Dr. Leslie White is the staunchest of the evolutionary anthropologists in the United States. He was trained in the Boas school, then taught at the University of Buffalo. While there, he discovered Morgan's work incidentally to his field trips to the Cattaraugus reservation. See White, "Diffusion vs. Evolution, an Anti-Evolutionary Fallacy," *American Anthropologist*, XLVII (1945), 339—56; "Evolutionism in Cultural Anthropology," *ibid.*, XLIX (1947), 400–413; A. L. Kroeber, "White's View of Culture," *ibid.*, L (1948), 405–15; A. R. Radcliffe-Brown, "White's View of a Science of Culture," *ibid.*, LI (1949), 503–12. Most recently the evolutionary approach seems to be gaining ground. "The problem is not whether there is progress but what it consists of," A. L. Kroeber, "History of Anthropological Thought," *Current Anthropology*, ed. William Thomas (Chicago: University of Chicago Press, 1956), pp. 293–312; R. Redfield, *The Primitive World and Its Transformation* (Ithaca: Cornell University Press, 1953), is an important recent attempt to rehabilitate evolutionary doctrine.

was hailed as a landmark in the history of ethnology. "I do not know of any discovery in the whole range of science which can more certainly be put to the credit of one man," wrote W. H. R. Rivers, whose own researches continued the work started by Lorimer Fison in Australia. But Rivers and most of his colleagues rejected Morgan's assumption that kinship terms reflect family structure. Until recently, Alfred Kroeber viewed the classificatory system as a semantic peculiarity. The monogamous family was not modern but as old as time. Morgan's and Bandelier's war on the Spanish chroniclers was justified, most anthropologists agreed, but Aztec culture was seen as far more advanced than Morgan would have admitted.[12]

In Europe, anthropologists paid more attention to Morgan's work, though estimates of it varied. The English historian of the subject, Alfred Cort Haddon, went so far as to declare Morgan the greatest sociologist of the nineteenth century, while Edward Westermarck, a Finnish ethnologist, devoted his life to disproving Morgan's postulate of primitive promiscuity. Believing monogamous marriage to be a biological phenomenon necessary to the preservation of the young, rather than a social custom, Westermarck denied that it was a product of historical evolution. But the distinguishing characteristic of European scholarship was its interest in the mythology of primitives and its habit of making institutions that Morgan regarded as economic and political into customs derived from fables. A view implicit in the works of John McLennan and Edward Tylor, it was

[12] W. H. Rivers, *Kinship and Social Organization* (London: Constable & Co., 1914), p. 49; Kroeber, "Classificatory System of Relationship," *Journal of the Anthropological Institute*, XXXIX (1909), 77–83; Alexander Lesser, "Kinship Origins in the Light of Some Distributions," *American Anthropologist*, XXXI (1929), 710–30; M. S. Edmonson, "Kinship Terms and Kinship Concepts," *ibid.*, LIX (1957), 393–433; Charles Gibson, "Lewis Henry Morgan and the Aztec Monarchy," *Southwestern Journal of Anthropology*, III (1947), 78–84.

enthroned in the massive writings of Sir James Frazer, who saw tribal structures and incest laws as a part of the savage's belief in magic totems and taboos. With the rise of psychiatry after Freud, European anthropologists increased their emphasis on the study of the primitive mind and especially on patterns of sexual behavior. Morgan's ideas came to be seen as old-fashioned and Victorian.[13]

Morgan held his own among a group of writers who made his name and Bachofen's synonymous with the theory of ancient matrilineality. Among the scholars who looked to this theory as a key to the Greek and Roman gentes, the most ambitious was the French novelist and philosopher, Robert Briffault. In 1927, Briffault published *The Mothers*, a rambling, three-volume synthesis of mythology, Morgan, and Marx that sought to trace the economic evolution of marriage. More precise in his employment of the theory, the English historian George Thomson partially rehabilitated *Ancient Society* by using it as a guide to a massive history of pre-Homeric Greece. Erich Fromm, recently convinced that Bachofen and Morgan proved the existence of ancient matriarchies, suggested that these threw new light on the Freudian interpretation of the Oedipus myth. A historical examination of the drama of Oedipus showed, Fromm wrote, "that the struggle against paternal authority is its central theme and that the roots of this struggle go far back into the ancient fight between the patriarchal and matriarchal systems of society." [14]

The posthumous career of Lewis Morgan reached a strange pinnacle when *Ancient Society*, the work of a

---

[13] A. C. Haddon, *History of Anthropology* (London: G. P. Putnam's 1910); H. R. Hays, *From Ape to Angel: An Informal History of Social Anthropology* (New York: Alfred A. Knopf, 1958).

[14] R. Briffault, *The Mothers* (3 vols.; London: Macmillan Co., 1927); G. Thomson, *Studies in Ancient Greek Society* (London: Lawrence & Wishart, 1949); Erich Fromm, *The Forgotten Language* (New York: Grove Press, 1951), pp. 196–212.

railroad entrepreneur and Republican, came to be viewed as a Socialist classic. Soon after reading it, Karl Marx died in London, leaving instructions for Friedrich Engels to acquaint European Socialists with Morgan's discoveries. "No less a man than Karl Marx," his colleague wrote,

had made it one of his future tasks to present the results of Morgan's researches in the light of the conclusions of his own—within certain limits, I may say our—materialistic examination of history, and thus to make clear their full significance. For Morgan in his own way had discovered afresh in America the materialistic conception of history discovered by Marx forty years ago, and in his comparison of barbarism and civilization it had led him, in the main points, to the same conclusions as Marx.[15]

In 1884, Engels published *The Origin of the Family, Private Property and the State*, subtitled *In the Light of the Researches of Lewis Henry Morgan*. Hailing *Ancient Society* as one of the few epoch-making books of his time, Engels outlined its contents and embellished them with material on early German and Celtic tribes, always distinguishing between Morgan's conclusions and his own. The American's virtue, he wrote, was that he reconstructed the main outlines of prehistory, stressing the primacy of economic organization. By proving that private property and the state were related in time and appeared late in history, Morgan had shown that both were only passing phases in the evolution of human society. Here Morgan and Marx agreed, and the implications for Socialists were obvious: "The society which organizes production anew on the basis of free and equal association of the producers will put the whole state machinery where it will then belong—into the museum of antiquities, next to the spinning wheel and the bronze ax." But Morgan had rushed in where Engels feared to tread. The disappearance of the state with the elimina-

[15] F. Engels, *The Origin of the Family, Private Property and the State* (New York: International Publishers, 1942), p. 5.

tion of private property was at conflict with the notion of a dictatorship of the proletariat, and smacked more of Bakunin than of Marx. It was a point that caused difficulties for Lenin when German Social Democrats, using Engels' book as a lever, attacked his theory of revolution. What Engels meant, Lenin maintained, was not that the state disappeared automatically with the establishment of socialism, but gradually, after the dictatorship of the proletariat had secured it.

In claiming *Ancient Society* as an example of materialist history, Engels was only partially justified. Morgan had, it was true, come in his own way to an appreciation of the importance of economic production in the history of society. The crucial difference between barbarism and civilization was in the transition from communal to private property. But the similarity of Morgan's materialism to that of Marx, striking as it was, ended there. With Marx materialism was inseparable from the dialectic. He saw the roots of social change in economic contradictions that tear society into classes. Morgan knew little of this and when faced with explaining the change from communal into private, and back into communal property, he saw the process as an idea implanted in men's minds. Thus, the sections of his book were entitled the "Growth of the Idea of Government," the "Growth of the Idea of the Family," and the "Growth of the Idea of Property."

Socialists of many factions followed Engels in his appreciation of *Ancient Society*. In 1891, Karl Kautsky translated it into German. August Bebel, in a work that was to go through fifty-one editions and that was eventually translated by Daniel de Leon into English, used Morgan's theory of the matrilineal gens to forecast the equality of women under socialism. De Leon frequently quoted Morgan in his writings and hailed him as a Socialist prophet. Because

Morgan's books became collectors' items by the turn of the century, Socialist publishing houses printed them in new editions. In 1918, the centennial of Morgan's birth, the *Weekly People*, organ of the Socialist Labor party, devoted an issue to his life and work. But by 1920, American Socialists also felt the influence of modern anthropology, and Morgan's writings, like Engels' *Origin of Property*, were referred to rarely.[16]

Still, a century after the publication of *The Origin of Species*, it grew obvious that evolutionary anthropology and Morgan's ideas had approached the end of their decline. As learned societies met to discuss Darwin's impact on various fields of knowledge, anthropologists were well into a general reappraisal of evolutionary doctrine. Scholars once virtually ostracized because of their belief in social evolution found more support among colleagues, and there were even signs that evolutionism was becoming fashionable. Whatever the outcome of the new debate, the values and the limitations of Morgan's contributions would be seen more clearly. Morgan expected and appreciated such controversy. Responding to the English taunt, "who reads an American book?" he wrote, in one of his last letters, that it mattered little who read it. American scholars must go ahead "and do even their own work over again in science, history and philosophy, and carry forward these subjects to their completion." In his view, he suggested, learning was not a quest for distinction or a search for ideology, but a voyage towards distant horizons of knowledge. He was too well aware of the pain involved in overcoming wrong

[16] K. Kautsky and W. Eichhoff, *Die Urgesellschaft* (2d ed.; Stuttgart: Dietz, 1910); A. Bebel, *Woman under Socialism*, Translated from 33rd German edition by Daniel de Leon (New York: New York Labor Press, 1904); *Ancient Society* (Chicago: Charles H. Kerr, 1910, 1912). More recently the Socialist Labor Party published *Montezuma's Dinner* (New York: New York Labor News Co., 1950). *Daily People*, September 6, 1905; *Weekly People*, November 23, 1918, November 22, 1919.

notions and time-hallowed traditions, but that made the journey more necessary. Like his Yankee ancestors, he knew it mattered less that for a time the course was lost, than that there was wind in the sails.[17]

[17] Morgan to L. H. Scudder, February 26, 1881, Morgan MSS.

SELECTED BIBLIOGRAPHY

Manuscript Collections

Hubert H. Bancroft Papers, Bancroft Library, Berkeley, California.
Adolph Bandelier Papers, Palace of Governors, Sante Fé, N.M.
Adolph Bandelier Journals, University of New Mexico, Albuquerque.
William Clements Bryant MSS, Butler Library, Columbia University.
Joseph Henry Correspondence, Smithsonian Institution.
Rossiter Johnson MSS, New York Public Library.
Edwin B. Morgan MSS, Wells College Library, Aurora, N.Y.
Lewis H. Morgan MSS, New York Historical Society.
Lewis H. Morgan MSS, Rush Rhees Library, University of Rochester.
Ely Parker MSS, American Philosophical Society.
Arthur C. Parker MSS, Rush Rhees Library, University of Rochester.
Francis Parkman MSS, Massachusetts Historical Society.
Henry O'Reilly MSS, New York Historical Society.
Henry R. Schoolcraft MSS, Library of Congress.
William H. Seward MSS, Rush Rhees Library, University of Rochester.
Lewis Selye MSS, Rochester Public Library.
Bernhard J. Stern Papers, in the possession of Mrs. Stern, New York City.
William L. Stone MSS, New York Historical Society.
David A. Wells MSS, New York Public Library.

Newspapers

Albany Argus and City Gazette, 1824–26.
Albany Evening Journal, 1860–61.
Auburn Free Press, 1824–26.
Rochester Daily Democrat, 1860–61, 1865–66, 1868–69, 1881–82.
Rochester Daily Union, 1853.
Rochester Evening Express, 1861.

PUBLIC DOCUMENTS

NEW YORK STATE. *Register*, ed. O. L. HALLEY, 1845.
NEW YORK STATE ASSEMBLY. *Journal*. 74 Sess., 1861.
NEW YORK STATE SENATE. *Journal*. 48 Sess., 1825. 91 Sess., 1868.
——, COMMITTEE ON RAILROADS. *Report of an Investigation of Alleged Fraud. . . . Senate Documents*, V, No. 52, 92 Sess., 1869.
——. *Report in Relation to Alleged Increases of Capital Stock of the Hudson River, New York Central and Erie Railway Companies. Senate Documents*, V, No. 58, 92 Sess., 1869.
U.S. BUREAU OF THE CENSUS. *Compendium of the . . . 6th Census of the United States*, 1841.
U.S. COMMISSIONER OF INDIAN AFFAIRS. *Report of the Commissioner of Indian Affairs*, 1861, 1862, 1863.
U.S. SENATE, COMMITTEE ON INDIAN AFFAIRS. *A Petition of the Tonawanda Band of Senecas. . . . Senate Documents*, V, No. 273, 29 Cong., 1 sess., 1846.
——. *The Case of the Tonawanda Indians vs. the Ogden Land Company. Senate Documents*, III, No. 156, 29 Cong., 2 sess., 1847.

LEWIS H. MORGAN'S PUBLISHED WRITINGS

"Aristomenes the Messenian," *Knickerbocker*, XXI (January, 1843), 25–30.
"Thoughts at Niagara," *ibid*., XXII (September, 1843), 193–96.
"Mind or Instinct: An Inquiry concerning the Manifestations of Mind by the Lower Order of Animals," *ibid*., XXII (November–December, 1843), 414–20, 507–15.
"Vision of Kar-is-ta-gi-a, a Sachem of the Cayuga," *ibid*., XXIV (September, 1844), 238–45.
"Letters on the Iroquois Addressed to Albert Gallatin," *American Whig Review*, V (1847), 177–90, 242–57, 447–61; VI (1848), 477–90, 626–33. Reprinted in N. B. Craig's *Olden Time*. 2 vols. Pittsburgh, 1848.
"Reports on Articles Given to the Indian Collection," New York University, *Reports on the Cabinet of Natural History*, II (1848), 84–91; III (1849), 65–95; V (1851), 67–117.
League of the Ho-de-no-sau-nee, or Iroquois. Rochester: Sage & Bros., 1851. London: Chapman, 1851. 2 vols.; New York: Dodd, Mead & Co., 1901. Rev. ed.; New York: Dodd, Mead & Co., 1922. New Haven: Behavior Science Reprints, 1954.
Diffusion against Centralization. Rochester: Dewey & Co., 1852.

"Athenian Democracy," *New York Quarterly*, III (October, 1853), 341–67.

"Laws of Descent of the Iroquois," American Association for the Advancement of Science, *Proceedings*, XI (1858), 132–48.

Circular Letter in Regard to the Possibility of Identifying the Systems of Consanguinity of the North American Indians with That of Certain Peoples of Asia. Rochester: Privately printed, January, October, 1859.

"The Indian Method of Bestowing and Changing Names," American Association for the Advancement of Science, *Proceedings*, XIII (1859), 340–42.

"Circular in Reference to the Degree of Relationship among Different Nations," *Smithsonian Miscellaneous Collections* (Washington: Smithsonian Institution, 1862), II, No. 10.

"Suggestions Relative to an Ethnological Map of North America," *Smithsonian Reports for 1861.* U.S. House of Representatives, *House Miscellaneous Documents*, LXXVII, 37 Cong., 2 sess., 1862, 397–98.

"The Great Indictment," *Rochester Daily Democrat*, May 16, 1865.

"A Conjectural Solution to the Origin of the Classificatory System of Relationships," *Proceedings of the American Academy of Arts and Sciences*, VII (1868), 436–77.

The American Beaver and His Works. Philadelphia: J. B. Lippincott & Co., 1868.

"The State Canals," *Albany Evening Journal*, March 12, 1869.

"The Seven Cities of Cibola," *North American Review*, CVIII (April, 1869), 457–98.

"Indian Migrations," *ibid.*, CIX (October, 1869), 391–442; CX (January, 1870), 32–82.

Systems of Consanguinity and Affinity of the Human Family. Washington: Smithsonian Institution, 1870. Vol. XVII of the Smithsonian "Contributions to Knowledge." Reprinted, 1871.

"Stone and Bone Implements of the Arickarees," New York State Museum, *Reports*, XXI (1871), 25–46.

"Oxford," *Appleton's Journal*, V (April, 1871), 497–98.

"Road over the Alps," *ibid.*, VI (December, 1871), 654–57.

"Australian Kinship, from an Original Memorandum of Reverend Lorimer Fison," *Proceedings of the American Academy of Arts and Sciences*, VIII (1872), 412–38.

"Instinct: Its Office in the Animal Kingdom," *Nation*, XIV (May, 1872), 291–92.

"The City of the Sea," *Harper's Monthly*, XLV (September, 1872), 481–501.

"The Human Race," *Nation*, XV (November, 1872), 354.

"Ethnical Periods," American Association for the Advancement of Science, *Proceedings*, XXIV (1875), 266–74.

"Arts of Subsistence," *ibid.*, 274–81.

"Montezuma's Dinner," *North American Review*, CXXII (April, 1876), 265–308.

"Factory Systems for Indian Reservations," *Nation*, XXIII (July, 1876), 58–59.

"Houses of the Mound Builders," *North American Review*, CXXIII (July, 1876), 60–85.

"The Hue and Cry against the Indians," *Nation*, XXIII (July, 1876), 40–41.

Ancient Society, or Researches in the Lines of Human Progress from Savagery through Barbarism to Civilization. New York: Henry Holt & Co., 1877; reissued 1878, 1907. London: Macmillan & Co., 1877. Chicago: Chas. H. Kerr & Co., 1910, 1912. First Indian ed., Calcutta, India: Bharati Library, n.d. *Die Urgesellschaft.* Translated by K. KAUTSKY and W. EICHHOFF. Stuttgart: Dietz, 1891, 1908, 1910. First Russian ed., translated by D. N. KUDRIAVSKII. St. Petersburg: L. F. Panteleeva, 1900. Second Russian ed., translated by M. O. KOSVEN. Leningrad: Institute of the Northern Peoples of the U.S.S.R., 1934. *Kodai Shakai.* Translated by K. ARAHATA. Tokyo: Kaizo-Sha, 1931; Shoko Shoin, 1948. *La Sociedad primitiva.* La Plata, Argentina: Universidad Nacional, 1935. *La Sociedad primitiva.* Mexico City: Libreria Navarro, 1947.

"The Indian Question," *Nation*, XXVII (November, 1878), 332–33.

"Architecture of American Aborigines," *Johnson's New Universal Cyclopedia.* 4 vols. New York: A. J. Johnson, 1874–78.

"Migrations of American Aborigines," *ibid.*

"Tribes," *ibid.*

"On the Ruins of a Stone Pueblo on the Animas River in New Mexico," Peabody Museum of American Archaeology and Ethnology, *Twelfth Annual Report*, II (1880), 536–56.

"A Study of the Houses of the American Aborigines with a Scheme of Exploration of the Ruins in New Mexico and Elsewhere," Archaeological Institute of America, *First Annual Report* (1880), 29–80.

Houses and House Life of the American Aborigines. Washington: Government Printing Office, 1881. Vol. IV of "U.S. Geological Survey, Contributions to North American Ethnology." Translated into Russian by M. O. Kosven. Leningrad: Institute of the Northern Peoples of the U.S.S.R., 1934.

Books

Adams, Brooks. *The Law of Civilization and Decay.* New York: Vintage Books, 1955.

Adams, C. F., and Adams, Henry. *Chapters of Erie.* Ithaca: Cornell University Press, 1956.

Adams, Henry. *The Education of Henry Adams.* Boston and New York: Houghton Mifflin Co., 1918.

Agassiz, E. C. *Louis Agassiz, His Life and Correspondence,* 2 vols. Boston and New York: Houghton Mifflin Co., 1893.

Bachofen, Johann J. *Das Mutterrecht.* Stuttgart: Krais & Hoffman, 1861.

Bancroft, H. H. *The Early American Chroniclers.* San Francisco: A. L. Bancroft, 1883.

Bandelier, Adolph. *The Romantic School in American Archaeology.* New York: Trow & Co., 1885.

Barzun, Jacques. *Race: A Study in Modern Superstition.* New York: Harcourt, Brace & Co., 1937.

———. *Darwin, Marx and Wagner.* Boston: Little, Brown & Co., 1941.

Bates, R. S. *Scientific Societies in the United States.* New York: John Wiley & Sons, 1945.

Bebel, August. *Woman under Socialism.* Translated from 33rd German edition by Daniel DeLeon. New York: New York Labor News Press, 1904.

Benson, Lee. *Merchants, Farmers and Railroads.* Cambridge, Mass.: Harvard University Press, 1955.

Berlin, Isaiah. *The Hedgehog and the Fox.* New York: Mentor Books, 1957.

Billington, Ray A. *The Protestant Crusade.* New York: Rinehart & Co., 1952.

Boas, Franz. *The Mind of Primitive Man.* New York: Macmillan Co., 1911.

———. *Anthropology and Modern Life.* New York: W. W. Norton, 1928.

Briffault, Robert. *The Mothers.* 3 vols. London: Macmillan & Co., 1927.

Burlingame, Roger. *March of the Iron Men.* New York: Charles Scribner's Sons, 1938.

Bury, J. B. *The Idea of Progress.* New York: Macmillan Co., 1932.

CHILDE, V. GORDON. *Social Evolution*. New York: Henry Schuman, 1951.

CROSS, WHITNEY R. *The Burned-over District*. Ithaca: Cornell University Press, 1950.

COULSON, THOMAS. *Joseph Henry, His Life and Work*. Princeton, N.J.: Princeton University Press, 1950.

CURTI, MERLE. *The American Peace Crusade*. Durham, N.C.: Duke University Press, 1929.

———. *The Social Ideas of American Educators*. New York: Charles Scribner's Sons, 1935.

———. *The Growth of American Thought*. New York: Harper & Bros., 1943.

DAMPIER, W. C. *A History of Science and Its Relations with Philosophy and Religion*. 3d ed.; New York: Macmillan Co., 1943.

DARRAH, W. C. *Powell of the Colorado*. Princeton, N.J.: Princeton University Press, 1951.

DARWIN, FRANCIS (ed.). *The Life and Letters of Charles Darwin*. 2 vols. New York: D. Appleton & Co., 1919.

DEWEY, JOHN. *The Influence of Darwin on Philosophy, and Other Essays*. New York: Henry Holt & Co., 1910.

DORFMAN, JOSEPH. *The Economic Mind in American Civilization, 1606–1865*. 2 vols. New York: Viking Press, 1946.

DUNLAP, L. W. *American Historical Societies, 1790–1860*. Madison: Cantwell Co., 1944.

DUPREE, A. HUNTER. *Science in the Federal Government*. Cambridge, Mass.: Harvard University Press, 1957.

EISELEY, LOREN. *Darwin's Century*. New York: Doubleday & Co., 1958.

EKIRCH, ARTHUR A. *The Idea of Progress in America, 1815–1860*. New York: Columbia University Press, 1944.

ENGELS, FRIEDRICH. *Origin of the Family, Private Property and the State*. New York: International Publishers, 1942.

FAY, JAY W. *American Psychology before William James*. New Brunswick: Rutgers University Press, 1939.

FISON, LORIMER and HOWITT, A. W. *Kamilaroi and Kurnai, Group Marriage and Relationship, and Marriage by Elopement*. Melbourne: George Robertson, 1880.

FLEMING, DONALD. *John William Draper and the Religion of Science*. Philadelphia: University of Pennsylvania Press, 1950.

FOREMAN, GRANT. *Advancing the Frontier, 1830–1860*. Norman: University of Oklahoma Press, 1933.

Fox, D. R. *Dr. Eliphalet Nott and the American Spirit. Newcomen Address.* Princeton, N.J.: Princeton University Press, 1944.
Frazer, Sir James. *Totemism and Exogamy.* 4 vols. London: Macmillan & Co., 1910.
Freud, Sigmund. *Totem and Taboo.* London: G. Routledge & Sons, 1927.
———. *Civilization and Its Discontents.* London: Hogarth Press, 1949.
Friends, Society of. *The Case of the Seneca Indians.* Philadelphia: Merrihew & Thompson, 1840.
Gabriel, Ralph H. *The Course of American Democratic Thought.* 2d ed.; New York: Ronald Press, 1956.
Gillispie, Charles C. *Genesis and Geology.* New York: Harper & Bros., 1959.
Gist, N. P. *Secret Societies: A Cultural Study of Fraternalism.* Columbia, Mo.: University of Missouri Studies, XV, No. 4, 1940.
Gooch, G. P. *History and Historians in the Nineteenth Century.* New York: Peter Smith, 1949.
Haddon, A. C. *History of Anthropology.* London: G. P. Putnam's, 1910.
Handlin, Oscar, and Handlin, Mary. *Commonwealth, Massachusetts, 1774–1861.* New York: New York University Press, 1947.
Haney, L. H. *A Congressional History of Railways in the United States, 1850–1887.* Madison: University of Wisconsin Press, 1910.
Harlow, S. R. and Hutchins, S. C. *Life Sketches of State Officers, Senators and Members of the Assembly of the State of New York in 1868.* Albany: Weed, Parsons & Co., 1868.
Hartz, Louis. *Economic Policy and Democratic Thought: Pennsylvania, 1776–1880.* Cambridge, Mass.: Harvard University Press, 1948.
———. *The Liberal Tradition in America.* New York: Harcourt, Brace & Co., 1955.
Hays, H. R. *From Ape to Angel: An Informal History of Social Anthropology.* New York: Alfred A. Knopf, 1958.
Herskovits, Melville. *Franz Boas.* New York: Charles Scribner's Sons, 1953.
Higham, John. *Strangers in the Land.* New Brunswick: Rutgers University Press, 1955.
Hindle, Brooke. *The Pursuit of Science in Revolutionary America.* Chapel Hill: University of North Carolina Press, 1956.
Hofstadter, Richard. *Social Darwinism in American Thought.* Boston: Beacon Press, 1955.

HOOPES, ALBAN W. *Indian Affairs and Their Administration, 1849–1860.* Philadelphia: University of Pennsylvania Press, 1932.

IRVINE, WILLIAM. *Apes, Angels and Victorians.* New York: Mc-Graw-Hill Book Co., 1955.

JAFFE, BERNARD. *Men of Science in America.* New York: Simon & Schuster, 1944.

JORDAN, D. S. *Leading American Men of Science.* New York: Henry Holt & Co., 1910.

JORDY, WILLIAM. *Henry Adams, Scientific Historian.* New Haven: Yale University Press, 1952.

KENDRICK, A. C. *Martin B. Anderson.* Philadelphia: American Baptist Publication Society, 1895.

KOSVEN, MARK O. *Materials for the Study of Lewis H. Morgan.* Leningrad: Institute of the Northern Peoples of the U.S.S.R., 1933.

KROUT, JOHN A. *The Origins of Prohibition.* New York: Alfred A. Knopf, 1925.

LILLEY, S. (ed.). *Essays on the Social History of Science.* Copenhagen: Ejnar Munksgaard, 1953.

LOWENTHAL, DAVID. *George Perkins Marsh, Versatile Vermonter.* New York: Columbia University Press, 1958.

LOWIE, R. H. *The History of Ethnological Theory.* New York: Farrar & Rinehart, 1937.

LUBBOCK, SIR JOHN. *The Origin of Civilization.* London: Longmans Green & Co., 1870.

LUNDBERG, GEORGE, et al. *Trends in American Sociology.* New York: Harper & Bros., 1929.

LYELL, SIR CHARLES. *Travels in North America in the Years 1841–1842.* London: J. Murray, 1845.

———. *Principles of Geology.* 11th ed. rev.; New York: D. Appleton & Co., 1877.

McKELVEY, BLAKE. *Rochester: The Water-Power City, 1812–1854.* Cambridge, Mass.: Harvard University Press, 1945.

———. *Rochester: The Flower City, 1855–1890.* Cambridge, Mass.: Harvard University Press, 1949.

McLENNAN, JOHN F. *Primitive Marriage.* London: A. & C. Black, 1865.

———. *Studies in Ancient History.* London: Macmillan & Co., 1876.

MAINE, HENRY S. *Ancient Law.* London: J. Murray, 1861.

MALINOWSKI, BRONISLAW. *Sex and Repression in Savage Society.* London: Paul, Trench, Trubner & Co., 1926.

————. *The Sexual Life of Savages.* London: G. Routledge & Sons, 1929.

MATHEWS, LOIS K. *The Expansion of New England.* Boston: Houghton Mifflin Co., 1909.

MAY, HENRY F. *Protestant Churches and Industrial America.* New York: Harper & Bros., 1949.

MERRIL, G. P. *The First One Hundred Years of American Geology.* New Haven: Yale University Press, 1924.

MORGAN, J. APPLETON. *A History of the Family of Morgan from the Year 1089 to the Present.* New York: Privately printed, 1897.

MORGAN, NATHANIEL H. *A History of James Morgan of New London, Connecticut, and His Descendants.* Hartford: Lockwood & Brainard, 1869.

MUMFORD, LEWIS. *The Golden Day.* Boston: Beacon Press, 1957.

NIEBUHR, H. RICHARD. *The Social Sources of Denominationalism.* New York: Meridian Books, 1957.

NOTT, ELIPHALET. *Counsels to Young Men on the Formation of Character and the Principles Which Lead to Success and Happiness in Life.* New York: Harper & Bros., 1841.

PARKER, ARTHUR C. *The Life of General Ely S. Parker.* Buffalo: Buffalo Historical Society, 1919.

PEARCE, ROY H. *The Savages of America.* Baltimore: Johns Hopkins Press, 1953.

PERRY, RALPH B. *The Thought and Character of William James.* 2 vols. Boston: Little, Brown & Co., 1935.

PERSONS, STOW (ed.). *Evolutionary Thought in America.* New ed. New York: George Braziller, Inc., 1956.

POUND, ROSCOE. *The Formative Era of American Law.* Boston: Little, Brown & Co., 1938.

RADIN, PAUL. *The Method and Theory of Ethnology.* New York: McGraw-Hill Book Co., 1933.

REDFIELD, R. *The Primitive World and Its Transformations.* Ithaca: Cornell University Press, 1953.

RILEY, WOODBRIDGE. *American Thought from Puritanism to Pragmatism.* New York: Henry Holt & Co., 1923.

RIVERS, W. H. R. *Kinship and Social Organization.* London: Constable & Co., 1914.

ROBINSON, C. M. *Third Ward Traits.* Rochester: The Genesee Press, 1899.

————. *First Church Chronicles, 1815–1915.* Rochester: The Craftsman Press, 1915.

ROGERS, W. P. *Andrew D. White and the Modern University.* Ithaca: Cornell University Press, 1942.

ROMANES, G. J. *Animal Intelligence*. London: Paul Trench & Co., 1912.

ROSENBERGER, JESSE L. *Rochester: The Making of a University*. Rochester: University of Rochester Press, 1927.

SANTAYANA, GEORGE. *Character and Opinion in the United States*. New York: Anchor Books, 1956.

SCHLESINGER, A. M., JR. *The Age of Jackson*. Boston: Little, Brown & Co., 1945.

SCHOOLCRAFT, H. R. *An Address Delivered before the New Confederacy of the Iroquois*, August 14, 1845. Rochester: Jerome & Bros., 1846.

——. *Personal Memoires of a Residence of Thirty Years with the Indian Tribes*. Philadelphia: J. B. Lippincott, 1851.

SEWARD, WM. H. *An Autobiography*. Edited by FREDERICK W. SEWARD. New York: Derby & Miller, 1891.

SHANNON, DAVID A. *The Socialist Party of America*. New York: Macmillan Co., 1955.

SIMPSON, GEORGE G. *The Meaning of Evolution*. New York: Mentor Books, 1956.

SMALLWOOD, W. M. *Natural History and the American Mind*. New York: Columbia University Press, 1941.

SMITH, E. PESHINE. *A Manual of Political Economy*. Philadelphia: Henry Carey Baird & Co., 1853.

SMITH, HENRY NASH. *Virgin Land: The American West as Symbol and Myth*. New York: Vintage Books, 1957.

SPENCER, HERBERT. *First Principles*. New York: D. Appleton & Co., 1864.

——. *The Principles of Sociology*. 3 vols. New York: D. Appleton & Co., 1876–97.

STEBBINS, HOMER A. *A Political History of the State of New York, 1865–1869*. New York: Columbia University Press, 1913.

STEGNER, WALLACE. *Beyond the Hundredth Meridian*. Boston: Houghton Mifflin Co., 1954.

STERN, BERNHARD J. *Lewis Henry Morgan, Social Evolutionist*. Chicago: University of Chicago Press, 1931.

STRUIK, DIRK J. *Yankee Science in the Making*. Boston: Little, Brown & Co., 1948.

TAYLOR, GEORGE R. *The Transportation Revolution*. New York: Rinehart, 1951.

TELLER, JAMES D. *Louis Agassiz, Scientist and Teacher*. Columbus: Ohio State University Press, 1947.

THOMAS, WILLIAM, JR. (ed.). *Current Anthropology*. Chicago: University of Chicago Press, 1956.

THOMSON, GEORGE. *Studies in Ancient Greek Society*. London: Lawrence & Wishart, 1949.

TYLER, ALICE F. *Freedom's Ferment*. Minneapolis: University of Minnesota Press, 1944.

VAN DEUSEN, GLYNDON G. *Horace Greeley, Nineteenth Century Crusader*. Philadelphia: University of Pennsylvania Press, 1953.

WADE, MASON. *Francis Parkman, Heroic Historian*. New York: Viking Press, 1942.

WARD, LESTER. *Dynamic Sociology*. 2 vols. New York: D. Appleton & Co., 1883.

WARD, ROSWELL. *Henry A. Ward*. Rochester: Rochester Historical Society Publications, XXIV (1948).

WAYLAND, FRANCIS. *The Elements of Moral Science*. Boston: Gould, Kendall & Lincoln, 1850.

WEINBERG, ALBERT K. *Manifest Destiny*. Baltimore: Johns Hopkins Press, 1935.

WHITE, ANDREW D. *A History of the Warfare of Science with Theology*. 2 vols. New York: D. Appleton & Co., 1896.

WHITE, LESLIE A. *Pioneers in American Anthropology: The Bandelier-Morgan Letters, 1873-1883*. 2 vols. Albuquerque: University of New Mexico Press, 1940.

————. *The Science of Culture: A Study of Man and Civilization*. New York: Farrar & Strauss, 1949.

WILSON, EDMUND. *To the Finland Station*. New York: Anchor Books, 1955.

YOUMANS, EDWARD L. (ed.). *The Culture Demanded by Modern Life*. New York: D. Appleton & Co., 1867.

ARTICLES

BANDELIER, ADOLPH. "On the Art of War and Mode of Warfare of the Ancient Mexicans," *Reports of the Peabody Museum*, X (1877), 95-166.

————. "On the Distribution and Tenure of Land, and Customs in Respect to Inheritance among the Ancient Mexicans," *Reports of the Peabody Museum*, XI (1878), 385-448.

————. "On the Social Organization and Mode of Government of the Ancient Mexicans," *Reports of the Peabody Museum*, XII (1879), 557-699.

BIDNEY, DAVID. "The Concept of Value in Modern Anthropology," in *Anthropology Today*, A. L. KROEBER, ed. Chicago: University of Chicago Press, 1953, pp. 682-99.

DEARBORN, A. S. "Journals," *Buffalo Historical Society Publications*, VII (1904), 35–225.

DEWEY, CHARLES. "Sketch of the Life of Lewis Henry Morgan, with Personal Reminiscences," *Rochester Historical Society Publications*, II (1923), 29–45.

EDMONSON, M. S. "Kinship Terms and Kinship Concepts," *American Anthropologist*, LIX (1957), 393–433.

ELLIS, DAVID M. "Rivalry between the New York Central and the Erie Canal," *New York History*, XXIX (1948), 268–300.

FENTON, WILLIAM N. "Iroquois Studies at Mid-Century," *Proceedings of the American Philosophical Society*, XCV (1951), 296–310.

FLICK, A. C. "The Sullivan-Clinton Campaign of 1779," in New York Historical Association, *History of the State of New York*, A. C. FLICK, ed., IV (New York, 1933), 185–216.

GIBSON, CHARLES. "Lewis Henry Morgan and the Aztec Monarchy," *Southwestern Journal of Anthropology*, III (1947), 78–84.

HALLOWELL, A. I. "The Impact of the American Indian on American Culture," *American Anthropologist*, LIX (1957), 201–17.

HISLOP, CODMAN. "A Loud and Awful Warning," *New York State Historical Society Quarterly*, XL (1956), 5–19.

HOLLCROFT, T. R. "Diary of William Fellowes Morgan," *Scientific Monthly*, LXXVII (1953), 119–28.

HOLT, W. STULL. "The Idea of Scientific History in America," *Journal of the History of Ideas*, I (1940), 352–62.

HUMPHREY, GEORGE H. "Changes in the Practice of Law in Rochester," *Rochester Historical Society Publications*, IV (1925), 203–11.

KOSOK, PAUL (ed.). "An Unknown Letter from Lewis H. Morgan to Abraham Lincoln," *University of Rochester Library Bulletin*, VI (1951), 34–40.

———. "Lewis Henry Morgan on the Flour Mills and Water Power of Rochester," *Rochester Historical Society Publications*, XXIII (1946), 109–27.

KROEBER, A. L. "Classificatory Systems of Relationship," *Journal of the Anthropological Institute*, XXXIX (1909), 77–84.

———. "White's View of Culture," *American Anthropologist*, L (1948), 405–15.

———. "History of Anthropological Thought," in *Current Anthropology*, WILLIAM THOMAS, ed., Chicago: University of Chicago Press, 1956, pp. 293–312.

LERNER, MAX. "John Marshall and the Campaign of History," *Columbia Law Review*, XXXIX (1939), 396–438.

LESSER, ALEXANDER. "Kinship Origins," *American Anthropologist,* XXXI (1929), 710–30.

LOEWENBERG, BERT J. "The Reaction of American Scientists to Darwinism," *American Historical Review,* XXXVIII (1933), 687–701.

————. "The Controversy over Evolution in New England, 1859–1873," *New England Quarterly,* VIII (1935), 232–57.

————. "Darwinism Comes to America," *Mississippi Valley Historical Review,* XXVIII (1941), 339–69.

LOWIE, R. H. "Evolution in Cultural Anthropology," *American Anthropologist,* XLVIII (1946), 223–33.

————. "Reminiscences of Anthropological Concepts in America a Half Century Ago," *American Anthropologist,* LVIII (1956), 995–1017.

LUBBOCK, SIR JOHN. "Systems of Consanguinity," *Nature* (London), XII (1875), 86, 124–25, 311.

————. "Ancient Society," *Saturday Review of Literature,* January 5, 1878.

LUMMIS, C. F. "A Hero in Science," *Land of Sunshine,* XIII (1900), 158–65.

McILVAINE, JOSHUA. "The Life and Works of Lewis Morgan: An Address at his Funeral," *Rochester Historical Society Publications,* II (1923), 47–60.

McKELVEY, BLAKE. "When Science Was on Trial in Rochester," *Rochester History,* VIII, No. 4 (October, 1946).

————. "Rochester: Political Trends, A Historical Review," *Rochester History,* XIV, No. 2 (April, 1952).

MANLEY, HENRY S. "Buying Buffalo from the Indians," *New York History,* XXVIII (1947), 313–29.

MANVILLE, RICHARD N. "The Fate of Morgan's Beaver," *Scientific Monthly,* LXIX (1949), 187–91.

MARSHALL, GEORGE. "Dr. Ely and His Adirondack Map," *New York History,* XXXV (1954), 32–48.

MOREY, WILLIAM C. "Reminiscences of the Pundit Club," *Rochester Historical Society Publications,* II (1923), 99–126.

PARKMAN, FRANCIS. "Indian Antiquities in North America," *Christian Examiner,* L (1850), 417–28.

POWELL, JOHN WESLEY. "Sketch of Lewis Henry Morgan," *Popular Science Monthly,* XVIII (1880), 114–21.

RADCLIFFE-BROWN, A. R. "White's View of a Science of Culture," *American Anthropologist,* LI (1949), 503–12.

RANDALL, HELEN W. "The Critical Theory of Lord Kames," *Smith College Studies in Modern Languages,* XXII, No. 1–4 (October, 1940–July, 1941).

RATNER, SIDNEY. "Evolution and the Rise of the Scientific Spirit in America," *Philosophy of Science*, III (1936), 104–22.

REZNECK, SAMUEL. "The Social History of an American Depression," *American Historical Review*, XL (1935), 662–87.

ROTUNDO, JOSEPH. "Eliphalet Nott," *New York History*, XIII (1932), 166–73.

SHERWOOD, J. B. "The Military Tract," *Quarterly Journal of the New York State Historical Association*, VII (1926), 169–79.

SIMMEL, GEORG. "The Sociology of Secrecy and Secret Societies," *American Journal of Sociology*, XI (1906), 441–98.

SMALL, ALBION. "Fifty Years of Sociology in the United States," *American Journal of Sociology*, XXI (1916), 721–864.

SMALLWOOD, W. M. "How Darwinism Came to the United States," *Scientific Monthly*, LII (1941), 342–49.

SMITH, VIRGINIA J. "Reminiscences of the Third Ward," *Rochester History*, VIII, No. 2 (April, 1946).

STERN, BERNHARD J. "Selections from the Letters of Lorimer Fison and A. W. Howitt to Lewis Henry Morgan," *American Anthropologist*, XXXII (1930), 257–79; 419–53.

———. "The Letters of Asher Wright to Lewis H. Morgan," *American Anthropologist*, XXXV (1933), 138–45.

———. "Lewis Henry Morgan Today: An Appraisal of His Scientific Contributions," *Science and Society*, X (1946), 172–76.

TOLSTOY, P. "Morgan and Soviet Anthropological Thought," *American Anthropologist*, LIV (1952), 8–17.

WALLACE, PAUL A. "The Iroquois; A Brief Outline of their History," *Pennsylvania History*, XXIII (1956), 15–28.

WATERMAN, T. T. "Bandelier's Contribution to the Study of Ancient Mexico," *University of California Publications in Archaeology and Ethnology*, XII (1917), 249–83.

WAX, MURRAY. "The Limitations of Boas' Anthropology," *American Anthropologist*, LVIII (1956), 63–75.

WHITE, LESLIE A. (ed.). "Extracts from the European Travel Journal of Lewis H. Morgan," *Rochester Historical Society Publications*, XVI (1937), 219–389.

———. "Morgan's Attitude Toward Religion and Science," *American Anthropologist*, XLVI (1944), 218–230.

———. "Lewis H. Morgan's Journal of a Trip to Southwest Colorado and New Mexico," *American Antiquity*, VIII (1942), Microfilm in Rush Rhees Library from the original in Marx-

———. "Diffusion vs. Evolution, an Anti-Evolutionary Fallacy," *American Anthropologist*, XLVII (1945), 339–56.

————. "Evolutionism in Cultural Anthropology," *American Anthropologist*, XLIX (1947), 400–413.
————. "Lewis H. Morgan's Western Field Trips," *American Anthropologist*, LIII (1951), 11–18.
Woods, C. A. "Some Further Notes on L. H. Morgan," *American Anthropologist*, XLVII (1945), 462–64.

UNPUBLISHED MATERIAL

Benison, Saul. "Railroads, Land, and Iron: A Phase in the Career of Lewis Henry Morgan." Ph.D. diss., Columbia University, 1953.
Butterfield, Margaret. "Lewis Henry Morgan's League of the Iroquois: A Bibliography." School of Library Service, Columbia University, 1936. In the Morgan MSS, University of Rochester.
Fuller, Clarissa P. "A Re-examination of Bandelier's Studies of Ancient Mexico." Ph.D. diss., University of New Mexico, 1950.
Marx, Karl. "Notes on Ancient Society," Russian translation. Microfilm in Rush Rhees Library from the original in Marx-Engels-Lenin Institute. Moscow, transcribed 1941.
Parker, Arthur C. "Biography of Ely S. Parker," unfinished manuscript in Library of American Philosophical Society.

INDEX